Dorchester Girl

By

Judith Kirwan Kelley

Dorchester Girl, published April, 2021
Editorial and proofreading services: Beth Raps; Karen Grennan
Interior layout and cover design: Howard Johnson
Photo Credits: Front cover: Girl's Latin School, Boston, MA: *Dorchester Reporter*, October 29, 2015 https://www.dotnews.com/2015/once-upon-time-there-was-girls-latin-school
All interior photos are owned by the author

 SDP Publishing

Published by SDP Publishing, an imprint of SDP Publishing Solutions, LLC.

The stories in this book reflect the author's recollection of events. Some names, locations, and identifying characteristics have been changed to protect the privacy of those depicted.

ISBN-13 (print): 978-1-7361990-1-5

ISBN-13 (e-book): 978-1-7361990-2-2

Library of Congress Control Number: 2021902061

Dedication

My book, *Dorchester Girl,* is dedicated with all of my love to my family. You are my heart for life: my beloved husband, Richard J. Kelley, Jr.; my daughters and their families: Kara and Madeline Katz; Lindsey and Vasudev Mandyam, and Malini, Raja, and Nayan Mandyam; Courtney and Ryan Viveiros, and Grace and Hannah Viveiros.

Acknowledgments

My book, *Dorchester Girl,* was an idea in my head from the age of 35 on. It took me until I was 66 years old to complete the writing and editing, since I seemed to talk about my publishing objectives more than actually write. Along the way, I had a variety of friends, relatives, and adult students who would query me about "how your Dorchester book is coming along." I'd shamefully admit that I was "working on it, but more in my head than on paper."

Over these years there were a few individuals who consistently reminded me that they were waiting eagerly to read my book, and to please "*finish writing it!*" At the top of this list is my friend of over 50 years, Barbara Jo Donnellan. Barb, or "Barbie" as I call her to her chagrin, has been steadfast in urging me to keep writing. She has the distinction of being the only person to have encouraged me to write (and praise my work) since we were both 14 years old.

Next on the list are a number of people who gently prodded me or answered questions to clarify faded memories. My sister Kathy Feeney, the one child older than I am in our family of seven kids, has been invaluable in providing me information from her genealogical research on both sides of our large, Irish Catholic family. She also helped me clarify information about memories that were a bit cloudy, but I could not find in official document research of any type. In exchange, I have left out all of our fights as kids, and how I loved to torment her by singing "*Freak Out* in the Darkness," instead of "Reach Out in the Darkness."

My late Aunt Pat Kirwan Kelley was the family historian, until I informally took her place after she died of a stroke. Aunt Pat was still telling family stories (often to our humiliation) even as she faded away into the arms of God.

A number of cousins have embraced my project and provided anecdotal information, entertaining enough to include in my book.

5

I got to delve into old stories with cousins Paul Sullivan, Connie Canavan, Jean Canavan, and Edith Canavan. Other relatives offered me titillating stories that, as entertaining as they may have been to me, I chose to leave out. I've thus omitted the names of these rumormongers in these acknowledgments, in order to avoid the fisticuffs that could arise as a result of certain revealed memories. You know who you are.

From College Hype, my absolutely favorite store in Dorchester and the source of my entire Dorchester and Boston Irish wardrobe, I especially want to thank Kathleen Dooley Hickey. Since the day I met her years ago and we talked at length about our beloved Dorchester, she encouraged me with the question, "Are you done with your Dorchester book yet?" She dangled the offer of placing my completed book in the shop for sale to all of the other Dorchester afficionados. Thank you, Kathleen!

I want to gratefully acknowledge my editor, Beth Raps, for her extensive work on my drafts. Beth responded thoroughly, but kindly, with encouragement and humor, and helped me to finally believe that I did have something worthy of publication.

For Lisa Akoury-Ross, the founder of what was initially Sweet Dreams Publishing, and is now known as SDP Publishing Solutions. The *sweet dreams* part of the original name absolutely captured my soul and I sought out her company for facilitating the publication of my book.

I am sincerely grateful to all of those, including my family (noted in the dedication of this book) who have been by my side as I have and continue to capture memories to preserve family history, as well as to educate and entertain. At least that's what my writing does for me.

Table of Contents

Introduction

I was born at Saint Margaret's Hospital in Dorchester, Massachusetts, on September 12, 1954. I have no recollection of my birth. I doubt my mother remembers my birth either, because she had been given drugs to have me—legal ones. In those days, women were sedated as soon as the doctor determined birth was imminent, which generally fell between his golf dates. The sedation period was fairly lengthy, with mothers regaining consciousness sometimes a day or more after delivery. Because of the drug-induced passivity of the mother, delivery of the baby was commonly assisted by the use of forceps. Typically, one of the doctor's feet would be pressed up against the end of the delivery table to help in the vigorous extraction of the bundle of joy. You might find this a far-fetched scenario except that I witnessed it repeatedly years later when I was in nursing school studying obstetric care and seeing first-hand this brutal practice.

Given that the majority of babies born in Boston in 1954 were primarily of Irish Catholic descent, obstetrics was a fertile field, in more ways than one, by which doctors maximized their incomes. Mid-baby boom, the years between 1946 and 1964 put a big bulge in the population. Following World War II, the United States grew by an average of 4.24 million new babies every year of that 18-year interval. This generation of "baby boomers" was also the result of a strong postwar economy, a time many American parents felt confident they would be able to support a larger number of children.

Aside from the fact that I was born during this population explosion, my birth was complicated in that I arrived during hurricane season. About 10 days before my birth, Hurricane Carol had struck the East Coast with 100-mile-per-hour winds on August 31, 1954. Naturally, my mother worried about how she was to get to the hospital with such troubling weather conditions. Her concerns were well founded. Rhode Island sustained more damage than Massachusetts; I came out as an eerie warning: one of the worst storm surges occurred at Point Judith in Rhode Island. I like to think that that was the origin of my name. In Boston, traffic lights, telephone poles, trees, and the steeple of the Old North Church came crashing to the ground. Approximately half a million people lost electrical power. My mother began to breathe more easily when Hurricane Carol abated over Canada on September 1, 1954.

However, she was not completely carefree about my arrival. Her previous delivery with firstborn Kathleen had brought my parents much anxiety. Kathy, a four-pound infant, was born six weeks before her due date. Kathy was not discharged from the hospital for six weeks post-delivery. Yet she had thrived over time and now—a mere 20 months later—the second child was due. The good news was that this second baby would not be premature and fragile, as Kathy had been. The bad news was that another hurricane was on its way. If ultrasounds had been in common use in 1954, it is likely that a smirk might have been detectable on my mischievous fetal face.

On September 11, 1954, Hurricane Edna blasted New England. Sustained 74-mile-per-hour winds hit Boston. More than 20 people died. My mother's due date was within the three days following the storm, and I left them scared silly about an unattended home birth if the hurricane didn't subside. I made it through the furious weather healthy and on time on September 12th. Relatives have teased me that my mother hoped to leave me at Saint Margaret's for a few weeks, as was necessary to do with fragile Kathy, but the nurses made her take me home. I was full-term and ready to rumble!

I have celebrated a number of birthdays during noteworthy northern Atlantic storms. In 1960, my sixth birthday took place as Hurricane Donna hit the East Coast, with wind gusts of 140 miles per hour recorded at Blue Hills Observatory in Milton. At six, what I remember is being directed by my parents to sit on the floor of the long, dark hallway of our Parkman Street apartment with my three siblings, Kathy, Jeanie, and Lonnie. The narrow hallway protected us from the violent winds because it was the only place in the third-floor apartment without windows that could implode in the storm.

My concern however was not the storm, but the far greater drama that my birthday was being overshadowed. I didn't get a freshly baked cake, or the presents I had anticipated since no one was able get to Capitol Market or Orbit's Department Store. I was so cross at being cheated in this way! But my mother just told me what the nuns at Saint Ambrose School always told me: "Offer it up to the souls in purgatory." That made me even madder! I wanted my promised blue plaid doll carriage with a Betsy Wetsy doll nestled among satin blankets. When I was close to being turned ass over teakettle by my father's hand (and not in the traditional, "birthday spanks" way), I gave up the fight, and was therefore allowed to live for my next birthday, and subsequent hurricanes.

1

A Formidable Father

Born the ninth of ten children to my emotionally distant English grandmother, Edith Kirwan, and my loving Boston Irish cop grandfather, Thomas Michael Kirwan, my father was emotionally remote with his children. Generally, he was not one to give or receive embraces, except where my mother was concerned. His own mother, "Ma," didn't hug, so neither did Dad. His father, "Pa," on the other hand, was a grandfather who genuinely loved children and showered us with affection.

As was the custom around Boston in 1951, my parents married at age 18 soon after high school graduation. My mother graduated from Dorchester High School for Girls, having earned what was fondly called the "Mrs." degree. The "diploma" for this accomplishment was the glittering presence on her left hand of an engagement ring. My father graduated from Boston Technical High School, also in 1951. They wed the following April in 1952.

My father and mother, Lonnie and Jean Kirwan, first lived on Faulkner Street in Fields Corner. By 24, they were the parents of three daughters and a son. By February of 1970 (when my parents were both 36), the family had increased to seven children (Kathy, Judy, Jeanie, little Lonnie, Christine, Scott, and Nancy).

My earliest memories of my father involve him working at Codman and Shurtleff in Savin Hill as an apprentice surgical instrument maker. He labored from 6:45 a.m. to 3:45 p.m. By then we were living on Parkman Street. Though he was the second youngest of his family of ten, he was the only one to earn a college degree. For many years during my childhood, he studied at Wentworth Institute, and then Northeastern University, both in night school. A maverick as an adult learner at the time, my father pursued his bachelor's degree in Mechanical Engineering. Weekends were sacrosanct for his studies, and his drafting table was always set up in the parlor.

He graduated in 1964 with his young family sitting in the stands of Boston Garden watching him walk across the stage to receive his degree. As a 10-year-old and an insatiable reader, I brought my new book, *That Damn Cat,* in my patent-leather Easter pocketbook. I read it from cover to cover during the three-hour-long event. I did lift my head at the designated time to listen for his name being announced, and to see him in his black cap and gown. I happily noted that the commencement program listed him by name, but I was nonetheless perplexed. It said that Lawrence T. Kirwan was the recipient of a Bachelor of Arts degree in Mechanical Engineering. I considered it for a moment, knowing that my father was neither an artist nor one who drove a train, but then I returned to my book. Dad was a college graduate at last, ambitious and exhausted!

My father was known by then as Lawrence Thomas Kirwan. He had dropped his original middle name "Jude" in favor of his confirmation name "Thomas" as his official moniker years before. And like my little brother, he was called "Lonnie" when we lived in Dorchester. (They both were called "Larry" once we moved out of the city, as my mother felt the change of names for both sounded less "city-ish." At home, my mother called him "Lon"—or "the old goat"—for the remainder of his life.)

During the years my father attended night school, it was my mother's job to keep the four of us (at the time) quiet while he completed his assignments. The easiest way for her to do that was to send us out to play. For children of that time and place, the streets were our primary playgrounds. We roller-skated, played Red Rover, hide and seek, Chinese jump rope, and standard jump rope (including Double Dutch). We bicycled to the Mary Hemenway playground, walked to Malibu and Tenean beaches, and made up games to challenge the rest of the neighborhood kids. One favorite of mine and the other scoundrels was to bounce our pink rubber balls off the steps belonging to the grumpy old man down the street who worked with my mother.

Never having had children, he and his wife had little tolerance for our shenanigans, and he would run out every 15 minutes or so and send us scattering. However, the angrier the neighbor got, the more enticing we found the game. We'd run away and hide from him, only to return as he closed his front door. He finally complained to my mother, who was furious that we had embarrassed her. My mother worked evenings with this neighbor at the South Postal Annex sorting mail during the Christmas card deluge. He had politely refrained from telling her about our misbehavior so as not to introduce an uncomfortable work situation. But once he could no longer tolerate our disorderly conduct, we were sternly prohibited by Mum from taunting this or any other neighbor! We responded to my mother's rare scoldings because if we didn't, we had to answer to Dad when he got home from work. The punishments from Dad, even if our misbehavior was less than egregious, were much harsher than administered by Mum.

During my childhood I don't remember fatherly hugs and kisses. But my father read to me. "Quoth the Raven 'Nevermore'" is still my favorite refrain. One of his preferred courses at Northeastern University was literature, and he passed his anthologies along to me to read when I was a very young girl. The two greatest gifts my parents ever gave to me were an endless love of reading, and the drive for lifelong learning.

My father was also a music lover and member of the Time-Life Book Club, which entailed receiving, for a fee, periodic hardbound collections in different genres. He played country and western music, classical music, show tunes, jazz, blues, and more on his treasured stereo. He sang along tunelessly but enthusiastically and particularly accompanied the country-western singers with self-taught lessons on his acoustic guitar.

Although my favorite music is Irish, my parents were late to fully appreciating the genre. We were raised in an atmosphere of cultural assimilation; immigrants to the United States and their successive generations were expected to meld as a unified America.

One of my father's favorite plaintive songs was "Goodnight, Irene." I hear it in my head as I write this. The song's origin is disputed, but most sources agree that the 20th-century American folk standard was first recorded by American blues musician Huddie William "Lead Belly" Ledbetter in 1933. I hadn't heard the song since childhood, when my father often played a variety of LPs during Sunday dinners, later strumming along in a valiant attempt at harmony. I thought I had forgotten it until I was recently gobsmacked with a potent reminder.

Among my favorite Irish musicians, the High Kings stand out. In late summer 2019, I purchased their CD *Grace and Glory*. To my absolute delight, I found "Goodnight, Irene" was on it. It immediately brought me down memory lane. I sang along with the lyrics without thinking, as I always had. Suddenly, as I gave voice to the last stanza, I laughed at the words I had once sung so blithely with my father. In the song, Irene's lover declares his limitless love, but ends the declaration that if she were ever to leave him, he would overdose on morphine and die.

It is, I admit, an odd and yet such a fond recollection. A father and young daughter, crooning along with a song about murder, morphine, and suicide. And yet I smile at age 65, thinking that those were close moments with my otherwise flinty father.

My father was more affectionate with my mother (as demonstrated by their having produced seven children). The deepest kindness I ever saw him show toward my mother came just before supper one winter night. Chronic nervousness (as it was considered then) plagued a number of us but was never acknowledged. Pain and suffering, for Irish Catholics, was meant to be "offered up to God and to the souls in purgatory." In other words, emotions were to go unexpressed, no matter how deeply felt.

Thus it was one day that my mother was in a visibly anxious state, pale and exhausted, while preparing supper for the family in time to have it on the table when my father sat down. As my father washed his hands in the kitchen sink, my mother lifted the completed meal off the stove, and shakily dropped it on the floor. The glass casserole dish shattered on the linoleum. My distraught mother burst into tears. We kids feared my father's verbal explosion. Instead, my father tenderly embraced my sobbing mother, then leaned down with a spatula and a bowl, and scooped up all the macaroni, meat, cheese, and sauce.

Terrified and confused about what was going on, we girls exchanged glances and tried to figure out what would happen next.

Young Lonnie just waited for his full plate. My father gently guided my mother to her seat and spooned the food onto her melamine dish. He nodded at us to indicate that we should all do the same for ourselves. Eating off the floor or the ground was an absolute violation of our sanitary code, unless we had "kissed it up to God, and spat down to the devil," as we did when we rescued gum or candy from the sidewalks. We kids ate in silence, still guardedly watching my father. We weren't used to less than strict adherence to established routines in our home. Still, he continued to make quiet conversation with my mother, while he encouraged her to eat. Still obviously shaken, she managed to get down a bit of the food. He pretended to relish his meal as she regained her composure. I've never forgotten that image of his gentleness when she dearly needed him to be that way.

My father, Larry Kirwan, was a successful man in so many ways. His achievements came not from the luck of the Irish but from Celtic stubbornness, and the ability to laugh and cry through pleasure and displeasure. In his lifetime, he had so much of both. Among his greatest pleasures were his wife, and my sisters and brothers and our families. And sometimes, his greatest sources of displeasure were his wife, my sisters and brothers, and our families. His joy came from having so many hard-won successes, and seeing his family prosper. His often-expressed frustrations came from what he perceived as our lack of adherence to a quest for perfection.

My father had an absolute credo: "Never accept mediocrity." He pushed us all to make the best of ourselves, and he let us know when we fell short. His criticism was always tempered with faint praise. Larry Kirwan was never one to mince words. With typical Irish diplomacy, he would say, "The only reason that I expect so much of you is that you have the ability to succeed. *Use it!*"

Kathy, the oldest daughter, had taken harp lessons for many years. As an adult she once transported the bulky instrument to my parents' home on Powder Point Avenue to reluctantly perform for our critical father. Kathy was somewhat nervous because she knew that Dad demanded a flawless demonstration, but she fumbled a few notes in her private recital. His assessment was after her years of lessons and practice, "Well, you've at least got the basics. ..."

From our early childhoods, we had seen him rise, and fall, and rise again, and give us our model on which to base our lives.

By Dorchester Irish standards, we were an ordinary family. By all other standards, my father was exemplary. Dad nurtured his career as my mother nurtured the family. Over the years, he progressed from a teenaged laborer to vice president of a major surgical instrument manufacturing company. Like the Jeffersons of TV fame, he was "movin' on up."

Our family relocated from Dorchester to South Weymouth on the Irish Gold Coast, and ultimately to Duxbury. As his family grew, so did my father's triumphs. However, his world turned upside down in 1978 when he was 45 and corporate changes left him unemployed. Through on-the-job training and the completion over time of a college education, my father ultimately ascended from unskilled 17-year-old laborer to the position of a vice-president when his employer came under the ownership of a major US medical/surgical company. It seemed that my father was now exactly where he had dreamed of being, in terms of career and family financial stability.

A short time after his promotion, however, a corporate shake-up resulted in the termination of the entire upper echelon of the growing surgical instrument division. My father, for the first time in his life, was out of a job. It was a low point for his family, and for my father's health. Within the next two years he suffered his first major myocardial infarction, or heart attack. He was very ill physically, but his Irish spirit ultimately won out. In the period of time after he was terminated from a job we considered to be the source of his success identity, he floundered. And yet during this period of profound depression and loss, he was carefully exploring his career options. He was determined to be on top again both career-wise, and status-wise. To my father, there was no choice. He would make it on his own. For his children, it was a significant lesson: You might be down but you are not necessarily out of the game.

I had slept at my parents' house on Thanksgiving eve in 1979. I awoke early the next day to hear my father crafting a rudimentary wooden sign in the basement. Getting up from the couch, I saw that his very own company—the New England Surgical Instrument Corporation—had been born in the night.

Very shortly thereafter, he had us all doing manufacturing piecework in the basement: We daughters were given manual instruments that looked like eggbeaters to form screw threads on metal blanks. But the two sons were provided with automatic medical screw-threading machines to do the same task more efficiently! At the time I was working as a Registered Nurse, and he quickly recruited me to travel from Boston hospital to Boston hospital seeking instrument repair work that he could do from home. From those he garnered some small contracts for surgical instrument production jobs and went from there to earning multiple patents on surgical devices, primarily bipolar coagulating forceps.

My mother, Jean, and my father rapidly developed the fledging company, soon manufacturing surgical instruments for microsurgical specialties such as neurosurgery, ophthalmology, and ear, nose, and throat. Initially the company was run from the basement of my parents' Duxbury, Massachusetts home. After a year of an increasing number of employees coming into and out of the suburban neighborhood, my parents decided to move the company to a bigger facility. In 1980, New England Surgical Instruments moved to an old shoe factory in Rockland, Massachusetts. It was there, in 1989, that New England Surgical Instruments became Kirwan Surgical Products. The new name helped the company distinguish itself from others and emphasize that Kirwan is a family-owned and -operated business.

My mother, Jean Kirwan, became President of the company after my father's death in 1996 and continued in that position until she died in 2013. The company thrives today in its second and third generation of family ownership. Family members in key positions in the company are two brothers and their sons.

As the company continued to grow, construction was completed on Kirwan Surgical's own 30,000-square-foot facility in the seaside town of Marshfield, Massachusetts. The company continued to grow in size and reputation, requiring two further expansions of the facility by 2020.

A side note about my father: He was a successful albeit misogynistic character. When the construction began on the initial Marshfield facility, one of the photographs published in the local newspaper showed the two toddler grandsons wielding construction hats and symbolic bronzed shovels, "breaking ground." I looked at my sister Kathy and said, "The die is cast. The future of this company is with the boys." It came to be.

Not to denigrate my father's grand achievements, and while acknowledging that he could not have accomplished this without my mother, his daughters were seen as minor players. At one point when he was suffering from congestive heart failure, I was at his home taking care of him and he got angry when he demanded that I make a phone call for him. I said patiently, "Dad, you are able to dial the phone. You should stay as independent as you can, even though you are ill." His face turned purple with rage as he screamed, "The girls in the shop would never dare to talk to me like that!" Through gritted teeth, I answered, "That is one of your problems. You cannot differentiate between your own daughters and your female employees." But I was at his house in the role of unofficial visiting nurse, due to my Registered Nursing license. Despite the fact that I was employed by Kirwan Surgical, I was still "just a girl." Ultimately, I did go back to working as a hospital nurse, my two sisters who were librarians returned to their respective careers, and the other two sisters resumed full time work outside of Kirwan Surgical.

As my father's health further declined, he became the not-so-silent owner. Even when he was not well, he made frequent phone calls to my mother and other family employees, demanding to know what shipments had gone out, and what orders and checks had come in. He never let go of his interest in and oversight of production and company growth.

He was eventually physically debilitated enough by heart disease to be at home, with just occasional visits to "the shop." But he made the best of those days at home, with his faithful Siamese cat, Ming Toy, and his two Shih Tsus, Suzie and Chu Chu, curled up on the bed with him. My father did allow himself one solitary drive early each evening; he and Suzie would go together to the local market for their earthly delights. He got a couple of cans of beer and a bag of peanuts. Suzie got a dog treat. This was a routine they looked forward to all day.

My father died a peaceful death after an idyllic trip to Hawaii with my brother Larry and his wife, Kung. He passed at home during the night, and by early the next morning, his wife, children, and grandchildren were all surrounding him, praying for him the eternal rest he so richly deserved.

2

⌘

Make Way for Mothering

Jeopardy held a significant time and place in my parents' lives. The time was 7:30 to 8 p.m. and the place was their bedroom, where my mother sat in her easy chair and my father lounged in the bed. No one was allowed to disturb my parents during their sacred practice of playing *Jeopardy* together. What emergency couldn't wait until 8:01?

My parents, despite all they'd been through together (or who knows? —maybe because of it), were fierce competitors at *Jeopardy*. (Serendipitously, my mother shared her birth name, Jean Currivan, with the wife of legendary *Jeopardy* host Alex Trebek. This may have given her an unfair advantage, but my dad never brought that up.)

As my parents aggressively attempted to match *Jeopardy* answers with their appropriate questions (according to the game format), each became more determined to win. They generally each held their own against the other, especially during the "Final Jeopardy" round.

Yet at some point, my father began mysteriously to call out the questions each night *before* Alex Trebek announced the answer. My mother became suspicious: How did he suddenly begin to win every night? Never one for sheepishness, he said simply, "I'm smarter than you." She knew that wasn't it! She soon figured out he had begun watching the evening's episode when it was first broadcast earlier in the day, so that he could cheat, and beat my mother.

That did not go over well. He was embarrassed to have been caught, and she was triumphant that she had discovered his ruse. But ultimately it just added to their mutual pleasure of this relaxing ritual at the end of a busy day.

There was so much more to my mother than her aptitude at playing *Jeopardy*. She was a spelling bee champion and known for being able to complete the *New York Times* crossword puzzle *in ink* without error! But more importantly than all of this, my mother was a proud housewife and mother of seven children. The term "housewife" has evolved to have such negative connotations. My mother was proud of her abilities on the home front, even after she had her consciousness raised by the feminist movement.

In my own early years of motherhood, my children never went to daycare. During the day, I was with my three little girls except when they were in school. Even then, I was class mother as often as the schools would allow me to be and chaperoned every nursery school field trip. In the evenings, I worked part-time as a Registered Nurse. So at those times, our roles switched, and Daddy was the happy caregiver of his three captivating yet conniving little daughters, Kara, Lindsey, and Courtney.

I was once in a bookstore with my three little girls when I encountered a woman I had known many years. She looked at me, looked at my kids, looked at me again, and asked incredulously, "What's a smart woman like you doing at home?" I was incensed! *I was doing what my own mother had done and I was raising my children.* While we might hope women would value other women's choices, there is a clear tension between those of us post-Women's Liberation who think it's a waste of time to be home with young children, and those who believe that leaving children in daycare to pursue a career is sinful. Suffice it to say, I appreciated having the opportunity to work part-time *and* be home with my children.

My mother demonstrated the value and obligations of motherhood. She molded us intellectually, behaviorally, spiritually, and with an appreciation for honest, hard work. She taught us social responsibility and the pleasures of cultural enrichment. If I said that she was no saint, I'd be lying. I'm no saint, and I'm telling the truth. My mother taught us moral values and expected us to follow her lead. The time my mother went shopping at South Shore Plaza in Braintree, she came home, looked at the receipt for her new shoes, checked her wallet, and determined the cashier had given her an extra two dollars in change. She drove the 25 miles back to the store and returned the money that, as she said, "didn't belong to her." I tried to rationalize to my mother that the salesclerk "gave" it to her, so it "belonged to her." My mother was horrified at what she saw as my lapse of conscience. Although she displayed occasional bursts of anger and other unpleasant human attributes, she lived her life by a strict moral code.

My mother had an erudite command of vocabulary and was proud of it. (Hmm, pride is one of the seven deadly sins. I've got her on that!) Traditionally, car salesmen have disparaged women's ability to make a reasoned car purchase. However, my mother had done her research and knew exactly what she wanted at the Lotus dealership: the Elan model. The salesman patronizingly said to my mother, "Good choice, young lady. The name of the car means 'deer' because it is fast and nimble."

My mother, although quite shy, was rightfully miffed, and instantly corrected him, "What you are referring to is an 'eland,' which is not actually a deer. It is an antelope. The model is 'elan,' which means elegant and graceful." She turned her back on his denigrating attitude, took her wallet, and went to the Mercedes-Benz dealership nearby. The respectful attitude of the salesman there helped ensure her purchase within record time. In other words, my mother got due regard (and a Mercedes S-Class) and the wise salesperson got a hefty commission.

Although my mother taught us all that we were Americans first and foremost, my sisters and I taught her to appreciate our Irishness. My reticent mother hated the stereotypical image of the drunken Irish, and associated them, as did many people, with the "paddy wagons." We brought her around to a love of Irish people and culture. She saw through the exaggerated characterizations eventually, and came to love the wit and wisdom, the literature, and the humor of the Irish people. In particular, my mother became a great fan of music from the Emerald Isle after numerous trips throughout Ireland with her daughters and granddaughters.

My mother traveled with various ones of her daughters and our own daughters both in the years in which my father was ill and after his death. The tradition had begun after my father had done what he considered to be an excessive amount of traveling for business. He didn't have the interest or the patience for leisure travel, but my mother loved seeing the country and the world. Together they proposed to the adult daughters that my mother continue to travel for pleasure, but that my father would stay home with nearby offspring to respond to his social and medical needs. When I was in charge of Dad, I would often get calls to "sneak him a six-pack and don't tell Mum." In the meantime, she got to see Rome and be part of the Pope's public audience, travel to China, repeatedly visit Ireland, England, Scotland, and Wales (the lands of our forebears), and visit out-of-state family members. Both my mother and father were delighted with their solution to her love of travel and his reticence to do the same.

Thus, it was ironic that my father chose to join my brother Larry and his wife on a trip to Hawaii in January of 1976. I insisted that I bring him to see his cardiologist for approval before he undertook the taxing trip. He was given the "good to go" by his trusted physician. During his stay in Maui, my father often telephoned home, describing the enchanting vista that he viewed from his hotel room. He was too weary to do any sightseeing but was also happy sitting oceanside puffing on a cigar as he enjoyed peoplewatching.

The three travelers had an uneventful return on January 25th, 1996 and my mother commented to us that despite the winter weather, my father arrived home wearing shorts, a Hawaiian shirt, and an overcoat in deference to the snowy day in Duxbury. He and my mother sat together and recounted his trip. A good part of the time that he was in Hawaii, my mother was in Italy with two of my sisters. She, as scheduled, returned home a few days before he did, and was there to share their vacation stories after she settled him into his comfortable chair with a warm meal. Travel-weary, they both retired early that night.

My phone rang at 5 a.m. the next morning. My mother's shaky voice uttered the words, "Dad is very cold. Do you think he is okay?" The 15-minute ride to their home was one of the longest of my life. Dad had indeed died in his sleep at age 62, after a glorious vacation with some of his adult children.

The deeply felt presence of God in her life and her children surrounding her helped my mother to survive my father's death. A funeral Mass was held in my mother's dearly loved Holy Family

Church, with grandchildren participating as altar servers and "carrying up the gifts" prior to the administration of Holy Communion. I wrote and delivered the eulogy, of course incorporating their nightly *Jeopardy* battles into the tribute to my father. As well, I spoke of the loss to our whole family of a cantankerous but caring father. I addressed the loss to my mother but assured the congregation that my mother would survive my father's death with the help of God and surrounded by her family.

The beautiful Irish song that most reminds me of my deeply observant Catholic mother is Carey Landry's 1944 "Hail Mary, Gentle Woman." The specific words chosen by Landry to honor the Blessed Mother of Jesus such as "gentle woman" and "quiet light" are particularly accurate in describing our own family's moral guardian. My mother continues to be, even years after her death, as in Carey's phrase, "Morning star, so strong and bright." At the same time, this song which opens with the phrase "Hail Mary" reflects my mother's lifelong devotion to the Catholic Church, especially to Jesus and his own Mother.

When my mother died in 2013 after a protracted battle with dementia and Parkinson's disease, she had been experiencing significant cognitive decline for many years. As it became apparent that she was approaching death, I sat on her bed with her and suddenly noticed that she had become lucid, if only for a few moments. I looked directly into her eyes and knew that she knew she was dying. I asked her, "Mum, are you afraid?" Her response was, "No. I am not afraid. I want to be with God and I want to be with Dad." Her words were a gift to her children. We grieved her death almost as if it was totally unexpected, but our shared stories of life with my parents brought us all a lot of comfort and plenty of laughter.

In fact, just a few days ago, even my mother's aversion to bad language became fodder for a joke shared with my sister. If we asked my mother for something that she believed to be unreasonable, her forever response was "Go jump in a lake!" More often, like her own mother, my mother often quoted lines from one of her many treasured books as responses to us, no matter what the question had been.

And finally, because my mother, like my father, passed on to our family an intense appreciation of reading, copies of my mother's favorite book, *Make Way for Ducklings*, were given to those who joined us at her final services, testament to her enduring love of Boston, and the story that she loved to read to her children and grandchildren.

With my own irreverent Irish humor, I love to tell people that my parents are my neighbors. If they know that both of my parents are deceased, they look at me quizzically, wondering if maybe I have more than a touch of memory loss. But I matter-of-factly clarify to them that they both still live on the same street as my own family, just over a mile down the road. Their final resting place is in Mayflower Cemetery, which is literally on the street where I live.

3

Kindergarten Days in Dorchester

In the 1960s in Boston, parochial schools did not have kindergarten. Instead, we all were sent to public school prior to entering first grade at Saint Ambrose (Catholic) School. Kathy, the eldest, went to Patrick O'Hearn Elementary School for kindergarten, located on the corner of Dorchester Avenue and Centre Street. Named to honor a former city building commissioner, and the founder of the Massachusetts Cooperative Bank in Fields Corner, the elementary school was a brick one-story structure built around an interior courtyard.

Kathy, born in January of 1953, arrived for kindergarten at Patrick O'Hearn each day wearing crisply ironed skirts and sweaters, durable but fashionable leather shoes, and lace-trimmed white ankle socks. My mother set Kathy's light brown hair in crossed bobby pins each night so that she wore the customary style of loose curls resting on her petite shoulders, neatly cut bangs, and a bright, shiny face. Kathy was always smiling, due to her ability to remain fairly oblivious to the three younger siblings who had come along as predictably as the trains pulling into Fields Corner Station. I arrived 20 months after Kathy's birth. Jeanie followed 18 months after my birth. And in November of 1957, the namesake son, Lonnie Jr., was born.

And then my parents took a sabbatical for seven years. We

three older sisters always attributed my parents' childbirth vacation to my father's relief after a son was finally born. Little Lonnie became the pampered prince to his doting parents and older sisters.

Christine and Scott, the fifth and sixth children in our family, were also born in Dorchester but were raised on the South Shore. Nancy, the seventh and final child, was born in Weymouth. By the time of Nancy's birth in 1970, declining numbers of our very large extended families still lived in Dorchester.

So the firstborn to leave the home for formal schooling was Kathy, the oldest and best-behaved. As my mother, with the next three in tow, arrived to pick up Kathy at the end of each session in her kindergarten year, teachers would approach. Repeatedly they praised Kathy's angelic looks and good behavior. And each day, Kathy smiled back. Through Kathy's graduate school days, her end-of-year reports from her teachers and professors were consistent: "Kathy is a delight to have in class!" She was always a hard act to follow.

Next up for kindergarten, I was sent to the Rochambeau School, in a Boston landmark Gothic building on Gibson Street. To say that I cherished my kindergarten year and my lovely, smiling teacher Mrs. Chippendale would be a vast understatement. Mrs. Chippendale exposed us to art and music, games, and co-operation. A lesson that has stayed with me for a lifetime was in botany

Along with our nature lesson, Mrs. Chippendale taught us a cute little ditty about a living organism with a furry silver-gray coat that lived in the meadow. The hook in the song was that we expected that this creature was a kitten, but one that, for some reason, could never escape from her sunny spot. To our surprise, we learned that we were singing instead about a plant called a "pussy willow."

Mrs. Chippendale then produced for us a large bunch of long branches festooned with these little furry "flowers." She passed around individual stems so that we could each hold one and lovingly rub in on our faces and arms. I was enchanted from that moment. To this day, I keep a large vase full of pussy willows in my kitchen year round, still singing the original song taught to me and my classmates by Mrs. Chippendale.

I introduced pussy willows to my own children and grand-children. Instead of the song that I had learned, with my grandchildren, we penned our own version of the Pussy Willow Song:

Catkins
Silver-grey nubs, known as pussy willows
Rubbed against my cheek like cozy little pillows.
Says mother, *Salix discolor* is the botanical name
But they're also called "catkins" for the short, fur-like mane.
I pluck a few nubs, tucking them into my hat.
I tell Mom I'm taking them home to grow myself a cat.
My mother smiles sweetly and tells me the news:
Pussy willows make no sound, you won't hear tiny mews.
Let these willows stay here in the meadow where they bloom
And a kitten we'll call "Willow" will snuggle in your room!

My kindergarten class made the *Dorchester Citizen* the day we churned butter. Just for us, Mrs. Chippendale had borrowed a butter churn, which consisted of a barrel and a wooden stave that was repeatedly plunged downward, thickening the cream to the desired butter. For city kids, churning with the plunger to turn cream into butter was a rare experience. I was chosen to deliver samples of our butter on saltine crackers to every teacher in the school. Carefully balancing the serving tray, I knocked on the door of each classroom and offered the delectable treat to each teacher. I reveled in the praise heaped upon me by the recipients.

What was it about me and butter? Family legend has it that I, at two years of age, would get out of bed in the middle of the night, open the refrigerator, and eat whole sticks of butter! My father resorted to tying a rope around the refrigerator at night to keep me from my midnight butter binges. Perhaps it was because, at home, white bread with oleomargarine was the standard accompaniment to our hearty supper, butter being a very precious commodity due to its expense. What little butter was purchased was reserved for our father (not the Holy One). Compared to the salty richness of real butter, margarine just didn't have the same cachet for me, even as a toddler. Oleomargarine, invented in the late 1800s, was originally composed of beef fat in a water emulsion. Modifications to make it more palatable meant that, by the 1950s, oleomargarine was primarily vegetable oil based. It was white and came with a dye that you mixed in to give it the yellow color of butter. Little Lonnie once swallowed the yellow dye and pooped the color of baby chicks for days.

Kindergarten for Jeanie was also at Rochambeau. But unlike Kathy and me, Jeanie did not find school enchanting! She perceived it to be unsafe without the comforts of her Mama. My mother dropped her off each day for the first few weeks of her half-day with Mrs. Chippendale. Petite and shy Jeanie cried . . . and cried . . . and cried. . . . Mrs. Chippendale would help to untangle Jeanie's octopus-like grasp from my mother, who was trying to make her way home with her now just one pre-school child. After four kids under five at her feet for years, this was my mother's chance to actually taste her cups of tea unencumbered by clingy little bodies. Lonnie happily toddled along beside my mother while Jeanie terrorized the other kids in the kindergarten classrooms with her ear-piercing daily shrieking brought on by my mother's departure.

Mrs. Chippendale, a seasoned early childhood teacher, naturally assumed that children beset by separation anxiety would stop sobbing and settle in as the weeks passed. That day came, and Mrs. Chippendale was relieved to hear that the last of the tiny tear factories had finally shut down: She couldn't hear Jeanie's whimpers. She looked . . . and couldn't see Jeanie either. Was it possible that she had settled herself into one of the little kiddy cubbies? But there was no curled-up child to be found.

In a panic, Mrs. Chippendale ran to the front door and found it open. She looked and saw Jeanie running full tilt down Gibson Street. Mrs. Chippendale gave chase and caught up with her just as she reached my mother and Lonnie at the Adams Street intersection. Jeanie was allowed to go home with mother and brother but soon returned to the classroom. Again, she cried.

In fact, she cried through high school graduation. I don't know why she always got so angry that I called her "crybaby Jeanie" until she was in college. In fact, she admitted to me years later that she had even cried in graduate school. But then again, I cried through graduate programs too, and I am not a crier.

My poor mother didn't fare much better when Lonnie went

to kindergarten at the Mary Hemenway School. My mother and our neighbor Mrs. Donnelly took turns walking Lonnie to school with Maeve, his buddy since toddlerhood. One morning, after Mrs. Donnelly returned home to tend to her two youngest, Aisling and Peter, then took a short trip to the corner store, she was shocked to find Maeve and Lonnie playing in the dirt in the six-foot-square patch of yard in the front of their apartment building! She wondered if she had forgotten to take them to school, but then vividly remembered strapping baby Peter into his stroller, holding Aisling's hand, and ushering Lonnie and Maeve to the Hemenway school. Apparently, the two kindergarteners had decided that school was not in their plan that day, and had simply left, finding their way back home on their own. They had clearly not gotten the memo: When you run away from school, don't go back home where you will quickly be discovered and returned to school posthaste. Both truants were told sternly to "wait till your father gets home!" The then-legal spankings would have taken place without either questions or the intervention of Children's Protective Services. At the time even the authorities accepted the dictum that to spare the rod was to spoil the child.

You might wonder why neither mother was worried about kidnapping. The neighborhoods were safe then, and it was not at all uncommon to leave small children unattended. In fact, when walking to Fields Corner or Codman Square with an infant in a carriage, it was commonplace to leave the infant outside in the carriage while the rest of the family shopped inside the stores. I never heard of anyone kidnapping a baby in the years that I lived in Dorchester. But then again, the last thing that one of the large Irish-American families wanted or needed was another mouth to feed, or more diapers to change. Furthermore, it was so unlikely that families had disposable income that no ransom would be forthcoming were a child to be snatched for profit.

4

༄

Fields Corner and Food

Woolworths had a lengthy lunch counter, where we spent many an hour and the less than one dollar that got us an entire lunch: soup, a grilled cheese sandwich, a drink, and a candy bar for dessert. My favorite part of the lunch counter was the bunch of balloons that hung tantalizingly above our heads. Woolworths had a constant promotion of "one cent to 39 cents" for a banana split. If you ordered a banana split (three scoops of ice cream, a whole banana halved and cradling the ice cream, three toppings on the ice cream, plus whipped cream and nuts), you'd choose one of the balloons. The waitress would pop your balloon and a tiny slip of paper would fall out with a price written on it: one penny, all the way up to the full 39 cents. Whatever amount was on that slip of paper was what you paid for your banana split. On multiple occasions—over many years, and many attempts—I scored a banana split for a penny. Along with a tummy ache, I also got to peruse the store on those days, after finishing my extravagant dessert, to figure out how I could now spend my remaining 38 cents. It was like a dream.

W.T. Grants had a vast candy counter where a salesgirl stood behind clear glass cases full of a variety of candies sold by the ounce. Grants's prices, appropriate to the families in this working-class community, were very affordable. And store sales attracted crowds. Very attractive promotions produced a plethora of customers.

One day, Kathy and I were in Grants when the candy counter began calling out to us. The special offer of the day was a quarter-pound of M&M's for five cents. We pleaded with my mother to give us each a nickel so that we could take advantage of this deal, promising to share our candy, and be conservative in our consumption. (Most of all, there had to be plenty left for Dad when he got home from work.) We took our coins and headed to the candy counter. My mother stayed nearby completing her errands while keeping an eye on us to ensure we didn't wander away. But we weren't going anywhere. We were each getting our own bag of M&M's!

We had some idea that the quarter-pound for five cents would be more candy than we had ever had at one time. Rules of the house dictated that all food had to be shared, so we wouldn't even get to binge-eat the quarter-pound of candy in each of our possessions. But the salesgirl pulled out a very large scoop and filled both lunch-bag-sized sacks to the top, and then charged us the promotional cost of a nickel.

We looked at each other, *pretty* sure that she knew what she was doing. Or did she? We estimated that we each had a full pound or more of the treats! We handed over our coins and walked away, unsure whether we had done something wrong or if she had. But we convinced each other we were not sinning because we had, in fact, each asked her for five cents worth of M&M's. We covertly tucked our bulging bags in our school satchels and walked home with our mother. When she asked if we had gotten our candy and reminded us to save some for the rest of the family, we breathed a sigh of relief, and thanked our lucky stars for a salesgirl with no mathematical ability.

My entire childhood, I was captivated by the candy counter. Years later as a teen, I got a job working behind the Grants candy counter in Weymouth. Yes, I did get sick of the candy with all that access to it, and virtually no supervision on my evening shifts. And it wasn't just the candy: As many times as I witnessed the open candy cases sprayed with pesticides, one would have thought I'd have lost my appetite. That never happened. In fact, as children, our practice taught to us by friends, was that it was permissible to eat candy found on the sidewalk if, as I explained in the chapter about my father's saving face the night my mother dropped dinner on the floor, one first "kissed it up to God and spat down to the devil." It must have worked. I don't recall ever getting sick after eating what was essentially garbage.

Henry's Hamburgers was the preferred spot for many of the Saint Ambrose kids who didn't go home for lunch. Besides the fun of eating lunch with your schoolmates, the quantity and quality of the food was unbeatable. Full-sized Henry's Hamburgers were 15 cents each, a small bag of French fries was 10 cents, a cup of Coca-Cola was also a mere 10 cents. Only 35 cents for an entire lunch.

We were out as a family one day, and my parents decided that we could get a half-dozen burgers (for a grand total of 90 cents), and a family-sized bag of French fries (59 cents) to take home. I was asked if we should get Coca-Colas from Henry's to accompany our meals. I was quickly told "no" by my mother, since we had plenty to drink at home. I went into Henry's to order, still scowling over the denied Coke. I got even angrier when the server called another, and said loudly, "Look at this pretty little girl. She looks like an angel, but she is *sooo* mad!" Their comments and laughter, though meant as a compliment, only made me more furious. But I felt justified. I *wanted* a Coke!

My parents rarely let us buy soda, or in the Dorchester vernacular, "tonic," primarily because money could be saved by consuming beverages that we had at home. Unfortunately, my creative and industrious father had had the idea six months previously that we could save a lot of money by not buying sugary drinks, but by him making them himself for family consumption. After reading a recipe for homemade root beer that my mother had found in the *Boston Globe*'s "Confidential Chat" column, my father decided to try it! He had the whole family save all glass beverage containers for months and then he sterilized all of the empty bottles to hold the bathtub full of root beer that the recipe made. He was so proud of that root beer. He even bought a bottle capper with which to attach the serrated-edge caps that would be fastened onto the vessels once filled with the syrupy brown liquid.

We were excited to make the root beer with my father, even agreeing to scour the bathtub to receive the unknown quantity that would be produced. The tub held a lot of root beer. The recipe made what seemed like a whole tubful. We all impatiently waited until Dad pronounced the root beer ready to test. He scooped out a cupful for each of us before taking on the time-consuming task of bottling it all.

I happily swigged down my root beer, and then gagged. I never was terribly fond of root beer, but the brown substance my father had made was completely unpalatable to me. I blame it on the sassafras in the recipe! Still, we were a family that didn't waste. Ever. We were instructed that, like it or not, we had produced over a hundred bottles filled with my father's freshly made root beer and we had to drink them all. Just the thought of root beer, and nothing but root beer to drink at home made me retch again!

Thus, when they sent me into Henry's to buy the family-sized meal, I begged for a Coke. I was admonished, "Waste not, want not." I wanted *not* root beer to accompany my take-out meal when we got home. The choice I was presented with was either root beer or nothing. I tried to figure out how long one could live without drinking anything, but I feared that my thirst would never out-last the tub full of root beer. I don't know if we, as a family every finished drinking all of that root beer. What I do know is that in the intervening 50-plus years between then and now, I have never even *sipped* root beer again. Not even a root beer float.

So many of my fondest memories are centered on food in and around Fields Corner: from Hi-Fi pizza, to fast-food and lunch-counter meals, to stores where you got rewarded with green or gold stamps based on the amount of your purchases. Once the stamp book was filled, it was redeemable either for more food or other types of gifts. I was so excited to find that the more we ate, the more incentives were earned.

There was also a delicatessen in Fields Corner near the Arcadia Street library. After returning my stack of books each week, and borrowing more with my tattered library card, I would pause in front of the deli before walking home. I was mesmerized by the commercial jars of pimento-stuffed olives and maraschino cherries displayed in the window. I figured out that if I kept winning one-cent banana splits and banked all of my extra 38 cents, in a year I could buy myself one of those huge vessels of green olives for my own eating pleasure.

Strangely enough, my middle daughter, as a young adult, had the same passion for a commercial-sized jar of maraschino cherries that I had as a child. One of her best friends surprised her with one of those precious jars for her 16th birthday. Fortunately, my daughter kind of likes our family, and shared her bounty with us. But family, please take note that I have still never gotten that coveted huge jar of Spanish olives!

5

Saint Ambrose Church

Acknowledged by many as one of the most beautiful churches in Massachusetts, Saint Ambrose was our first family church. Although my parents were married at Saint Leo's Church in Dorchester, by the time the first four of seven children came along, we were parishioners at Saint Ambrose.

Saint Ambrose parish was founded by Father John Harrigan on December 7, 1914—the feast day of Saint Ambrose. This was in response to the rapidly growing population in the district, especially of Irish immigrants and their families. By November 1915, the construction of the lower church was completed and ready for occupancy. The lower church accommodated 1200 parishioners and was fitted with a large central altar and two small upper altars. A choir loft held 50 additional parishioners. All church services were held in the lower church until the expansion of the parish necessitated the building of the upper church. Construction began in 1920 and was completed a year later. The upper church held an additional 1400 people. His Eminence Cardinal William Henry O'Connell blessed the completed upper church.

Constructed of Barrington red brick and trimmed with granite in the English Gothic style, the church resembled Notre Dame Cathedral with its twin towers in the front. Three elegant doors in each of which were set six stained-glass panels led into the front of the church. The center aisle led to the main altar of Italian Carrara marble, considered to be one of the most breathtaking in the entire country.

Over the main altar was a grand stained-glass window depicting the Last Supper. To the left and right of the main altar were stained-glass windows representing the birth of Christ and the Resurrection. On each side of the church were five stained-glass windows portraying Christ ministering to the people. The windows were created in and imported from Munich.

In 1929 the rectory was completed. The red brick Saint Ambrose School was built in 1936 behind the rectory on Leonard Street. The convent for the teaching Sisters of Saint Joseph was built in 1942.

Our family were parishioners at Saint Ambrose from the early 1950s. Jeanie, Lonnie, and I were all baptized at Saint Ambrose. We all made our First Confession and First Communion at Saint Ambrose, but Kathy was the only one to graduate from the school. I went to Saint Ambrose from first to fifth grades, and then we moved from Parkman to Edwin Street and became part of Saint Mark's parish. However, Saint Ambrose School continues to hold a very special place in my heart.

In 1984, I was 30 years old, living in Marshfield, Massachusetts, and a parishioner at Saint Christine's Church. I was working at South Shore Hospital in Weymouth as a Registered Nurse when, on the way to work on Wednesday, January 25th, I heard devastating news on WBZ radio: Saint Ambrose Church had burnt down the previous evening. Not quite at the hospital yet for my 3 p.m. shift, I pulled my car to the side of the road, and I cried. I listened to and watched every newscast I could to find out what had happened. The church fire was believed to have been arson, and while there was a suspect, there was never a conviction. Investigators determined that fire had erupted in the sanctuary around 8 p.m. A burglary attempt had taken place in the basement of the church, where a safe was found empty.

Despite a quick, nine-alarm response from the fire department, the roof of the church was destroyed, leaving the structure precarious. As the fire blazed, the pastor of Saint Ambrose, Reverend Paul Clougherty, firefighters, and parishioners risked their lives to carry sacred objects, statues, and other artifacts from the church. The Holy Eucharist, the symbolic body of Jesus Christ, was also saved from the ravages of the fire.

After the fire, a church rebuilding fund allowed for a new red brick and granite church in the English Gothic style to be built. The new church, instead of having twin towers was constructed with a central tower surrounded by pinnacles. Many of the new building's windows utilized stained glass salvaged from the partially destroyed original windows. Considered by the faithful to be nothing short of a miracle, the original stained-glass window of the Last Supper was one of those saved in the fire and is now positioned just behind the altar in the new church, just as it was in the old church. Another window depicting Christ blessing Saint Peter was also salvaged and placed in the new tower, capped by pinnacles saved from the original towers.

Of significance is that these two stained-glass windows were saved by the efforts of firefighters who included Stephen Minehan who grew up in the parish and attended Saint Ambrose School. Minehan graduated in 1964, married and raised four children. Firefighter Minehan later died fighting a blaze in a vacant Charlestown warehouse on the night of June 24, 1994. On April 24, 1996, the Saint Ambrose School hall was named in his memory in a ceremony attended by the Boston Fire Department.

Saint Ambrose parish was initially formed to meet the spiritual needs of primarily Irish immigrants and their descendants. Today Saint Ambrose parish is home to a vibrant, ethnically diverse Roman Catholic community who come primarily from the Dominican Republic, Guatemala, Honduras, Ireland, and Vietnam.

6

Urgency and the Alphabet Game

Two consistent problems I had with lengthy church services in childhood were bladder frequency and boredom. The physical discomfort was far more vexing than the tedium.

As soon as I was taught to "hold it," I found that I often couldn't. If I managed to, it was either with the help of the seated "pee-pee dance" that would get me a knuckle rap on the head, or with a lot of frantic urethral clenching. The second was more subtle but definitely less comfortable.

"Bladder frequency," defined as having the urge to void more than six to seven times within a 24-hour period, is a family trait, except for one of my sisters, who could put a camel to shame with her exceptional bladder capacity.

A contributing factor to my intense discomfort was that Catholic churches gave far more attention to spiritual needs than physical ones. As a child, I didn't even know if there *were* toilets anywhere in church buildings. We were never advised what to do if we had pressing urges during services, and if we voiced any complaint of discomfort to the nuns, we would be told to "offer it up to the souls in Purgatory."

As it often was, I had something to "do" and no place to "go." So, I suffered. After being in church for more than 20 minutes, I felt the necessity. I could pass it off for a while, but as services continued, I became more uncomfortable, until finally I was writhing in pain with bladder pressure to the point that I had tears in my eyes. This is not to be confused with the Irish expression that "your bladder is too close to your eyes," meaning that you cry too easily. Instead, I think the excess bodily fluid was just looking for a place from which to escape.

In a panic, I thought of ways the problem could be addressed, as this was a chronic situation for me. I considered surreptitiously borrowing a diaper or two from one of the babies in our family. But disposables weren't yet available. The thoughts of a bulky cotton nappy wrapped around my ample rump, and then covered in rubber pants, was too embarrassing to consider. Finally, though, I saw the solution! If only there could be a slender tube that drained the urine out of my bursting bladder and conveyed it into a holding receptacle attached to my thigh for later emptying. There *was* such a thing, but I had no knowledge of the Foley indwelling catheter at the time, even though it had been invented in 1929. As well, I didn't know how placement would occur as I had little to no knowledge of parts of my body that were considered private. They were too private for me to even think about. Instead, I suffered in silence and ran to the closest bathroom once we were released from church services. It was a desperate race each and every time.

This was also a problem in schools for many years. When I was a child, there was an established lavatory break each morning, where girls and boys would be escorted by the teachers to the appropriate bathrooms. There was no such corollary event in the afternoons, after lunch. The only hope was that one who could leave school for lunch also got an after-meal potty opportunity. There were no scheduled afternoon bathroom breaks anywhere I went to school from elementary school through high school. Modesty was taught as a virtue, but it was actually quite a hindrance to physical need and comfort.

I was so aware of the distress that need to use the bathroom caused that when my own children went to school I wrote letters to each of their teachers requesting that they let my children use the bathroom when they asked to do so. I instructed my children that if they were denied permission, then they were to simply leave the room to go to the bathroom. There were a few teachers that argued with my requests to honor my children's needs. I made it clear to such individuals that I would address the issue in person, and possibly in court, should any of my children or other children embarrass themselves by wetting their pants in class because of a refusal of permission to attend to bodily needs. When you gotta go, you gotta go!

I don't know when toilets in churches came into being, but nowadays I immediately ascertain the location of the nearest bathrooms in whichever church I am in at the time. If the need arises, so do I. A simple whispered "excuse me" to the people whom I might climb over to get to the toilet is typically all it takes. And now if I could only convince the priests to let me bring my Dunkin' Donuts coffee with me into Mass.

Boredom was my other problem with church when I was a child (and sometimes even now). As Catholic children, we spent many hours in church: for Confession, for Sunday Mass, for Holy Days of Obligation Masses, for First Friday Masses, for Lenten Services, and for Stations of the Cross, among other Catholic requirements. If nuns or our parents observed our signs of impatience with humdrum homilies, we would be physically reprimanded. From the nuns, it was usually a knock to our heads to grab our attention, followed by a stern warning to keep our eyes ahead and on the services. From my mother, if we acted up anywhere as kids, we got the "monkey bite," a painful pinch on the soft skin on the underside of our upper arms. If my mother pinched (and she pinched hard enough to leave bruises), and we responded vocally, we got another, harder, pinch.

I loved the Latin Mass, and could understand the prayers, and recite the appropriate responses with the best of them, so it wasn't lack of familiarity. It was simple tedium. The situation never changed when the Mass began to be said in English after Vatican II. Boredom was boredom in any language.

So, I developed a solution to my problem which made the time in church fly by. An added bonus was that it distracted me from my bladder discomfort. I invented a game that required no other materials than my daily Missal. The game was quiet and solitary, and made it appear that I was paying rapt attention to the Mass. The rules of my game were as follows:

1. Select a Gospel or other reading or prayer equivalent to at least a full paragraph of text.

2. Starting at the beginning of the reading, look for each letter of the alphabet the first time it appeared.

3. When letter "A" had been found, start again at the beginning of the same reading, and look for the first occurrence of each subsequent letter of the alphabet

4. Continue until the first occurrences of all 26 letters of the alphabet had been located. (If this occurred, it was a "win.")

5. If a letter did not appear anywhere in the reading, begin the game again with a new reading.

6. If there was no time to begin anew, quantify success or failure: e.g., what percentage of letters *had* been located, in order? If only one letter was missing, I could declare myself "runner-up" to myself. It was my game and thus, my rules.

Example: If it were a brief Mass (which rarely happened), I might substitute a commonly said prayer from our 1960s missals such as the "Our Father," rather than the designated reading for that day. Application of my devised rules would be as follows:

"**Our Father, W**ho art in heaven, hallowe**d be** Thy name; Thy **k**ingdom come; Thy will be done on earth as it is in heaven. Give us this day our daily bread; and forgive us our trespasses as we forgive those who trespass against us: and lead us not into temptation but deliver us from evil. Amen."

As is seen, none of the following letters are found in the "Our Father:" *J, Q, X,* or *Z.* In fact, these are four least common letters in the English language. If I located all 26 letters of the alphabet in my random selection, I scored myself a winner. My score in the "Our Father" would be 22 letters out of 26—to me, an average score. If I cheated (in church!) at my own game and pre-screened the game prayers or readings for the letters *J, Q, X,* and *Z,* I enhanced my chances of a perfect score. For instance, the rare reading that might include *Jesus, queen, oxen,* and *Ezekiel* in the same reading would be a stolen victory, but a victory nonetheless. That would complete a full set of 26 letters of the alphabet! My quest for perfection compelled me, I am embarrassed to admit, to sometimes actually cheat on my own game. I allowed my obsessive-compulsive tendencies to justify that if I didn't take a few liberties in order to wrap up the game, that I would never leave the church that day until I was "successful" in completing my self-given task.

I should not be proud that I taught my own three daughters my game when they were still faithfully attending Mass as parochial school students. But in my defense, my device prevented me from ever getting a call from the nuns that any of my daughters had been distracting others during services. Their heads were bent over their Holy Missals, fingers tracing the letters, lips moving: What more evidence might there be of total devotion to Mass? Whereas a fist pumped in victory and an unsuppressed cheer upon finding all 26 letters of the alphabet in one game would likely have been a clue to the nuns that malfeasance was at play.

7

Memories of My Years at Saint Ambrose School

The nuns of my childhood initially seemed to be benevolent creatures of God. I had been introduced to them at Children's Masses in the lower church of Saint Ambrose School. Saint Ambrose had a rigorous routine for its children of their entering the school in morning formation and exiting at the end of the day accompanied by military music, including "The Caissons Go Rolling Along," and "The Saints Go Marching In." I couldn't wait to be a part of this pomp and circumstance, centered around Sister Mary Saint Luke as Kathy's first-grade teacher. Our whole family came to know Sister Mary Saint Luke as a petite but fierce woman. She was hardly taller than her first-grade students, but she had a ferocious temper. In Irish parlance, Sister Saint Luke was "she who must be obeyed!"

Sweet Kathy easily fell into line in Sister Saint Luke's classroom, and we rarely heard a complaint from my older sister about her teacher. The few times Kathy got into trouble with Sister Saint Luke were for napping at her desk instead of practicing silent reading, napping in the "basement" (the name we were told to call the bathroom, for some reason), and finding a quiet corner of the playground for a catnap while other first-graders were jumping rope. If, at the time, her teacher was traumatizing others, Kathy was likely oblivious to it, and more concerned about the possibility of another nap when Sister was otherwise distracted.

However, even at my young age of three, I had a jaundiced eye, and closely watched the minute menace of Saint Ambrose's first grade, knowing that my day was coming. Kathy entered first grade in 1958. I followed in 1960. Although I was well behaved by parental demand, I took close note of the fates befalling those who chose to defy the commands of our first-grade nun. I saw clearly that Sister Saint Luke induced fear in people small and large, young and old. Sister Saint Luke had earned her 40-year reputation as a Tasmanian devil. Merely saying her name in a crowd in Fields Corner caused people to scurry and seek sanctuary.

The September day we entered Class 1A, Sister Saint Luke took us all emotional hostage. Barking while pointing her bony finger at designated chairs, she assigned us to our respective seats. Those who did not drop quickly enough into the wooden chairs were shoved into place. Rapidly we learned that if we did not respond loudly enough as a class to her "Good morning, children" with a hearty but respectful, "Good morning, Sister Mary Saint Luke," one or more children would be locked in the cloakroom for hours. The wide coat closet spanned the entire back of the classroom. If you opened or closed one section, all sections opened or closed. The dreaded cloakroom was dark until opened and could hold many children at once. To be honest, I don't recall Sister Saint Luke actually locking up more than a few children at a time . . . a long time. Sometimes she forgot that she had put a child into the cloakroom when she felt that the child had been deliberately unruly (for example, a child who sneezed). But we children were too frightened to knock from inside the folding door to remind her of our presence.

It was not uncommon for a child to finally be released in tears and with wet underwear. Wet underpants were handled matter-of-factly, as they were a common occurrence. Underpants were removed and placed on radiators, filling the classroom with the aroma of warm urine, then returned to the child to be put back on. There were typically three or four pair of undies on the heater, and occasionally boys' long pants as well. Sister kept used children's underwear in her closet so that no child was ever humiliated before God by being naked below, on top of their public humiliation.

Sister Saint Luke was mean to girls, but she took a particular delight in treating little boys with abject cruelty. Her beady eyes would peruse the room, just waiting to catch Brian or Brendan, Peter or Paul, with a finger up his nose. If she caught a picker in action, she pounced. For this offense, Sister Saint Luke kept a box full of dirty rags in the coat closet. To mark his shame, Sister Saint Luke would pin the biggest, filthiest, torn piece of fabric to the front of his white dress shirt. Little boys cried. Little girls sobbed even harder, because the boys were crying. The offender was made to wear the mark of the nosepicker all day. Although we cringed in empathetic shame, we dared not show it. Those whom Sister Saint Luke perceived to be traitors to her ended up in the cloakroom.

Sister Saint Luke was like a wild bird in flight. A child never knew where she would light next, having observed some miscreant whom she believed deserved her harsh corrective measures. We were instructed to never look toward Sister Saint Luke as she moved quickly and quietly around the classroom, seeking out behavior that she counted as sinful. She would call out, "Eyes to the front!" and only the hardiest of souls would dare to peek to see where Sister was skulking. Soon, however, we would see her puny fist grasping the ear of a child as she dragged them toward her desk where punishment would be meted out. Most often, it was a little boy, as, in her words, they were acting "Satan-like."

Our old school building had large, airy, high-ceilinged class-rooms. The windows facing Leonard Street could only be opened and closed by one of the taller boys armed with a six-foot-long hook, designed for operating the mechanical window locks. A chalkboard extended the entire length of the front of the room, framed underneath by the chalk and eraser ledge. Walls were painted a sickly pale green, after research had, at some point, revealed that this was the color most conducive to learning. Of primary interest to the students, then and now, were the clocks. Millions of schoolchildren everywhere have spent countless hours intended for lessons instead focusing on the extraordinarily slow-moving hands of school clocks as they tick away the school day.

When Sister dragged young boys to the front of the room, it was often following her threat to hang them from the lights. The room lights dangled from wire cables attached to the high ceilings. Dark green semi-spherical shades directed the light downwards, but the exposed bulbs harshly glared. The entire fixture dropped from ceiling level to less than six feet from the floor.

At the time, the Saint Ambrose boys were required to wear ironed and starched, long-sleeved white dress shirts, navy blue trousers, and navy blue ties. The traditional Windsor knot was most often tied by the boy's mother until he came of age to do it himself. Had the mothers ever anticipated how their sons' ties might be used, they might have refused to accessorize their sons as required.

Worn correctly, the tie knot served to secure the noose by which Sister Saint Luke threatened daily to hang some young man from the light fixture. Sister Saint Luke believed that this served both as sufficient punishment to a perceived offender, as well as deterrence to other misbehaving boys.

While this member of the Sisters of Saint Joseph plied her trade as an educator of young minds, she served also as an arm of the law. Her law. As the habit-clad little nun yanked the child by the tie, she pulled it upwards. Frightened and sympathetic classmates cried, begging Sister to stop. "Please, Sista," we would beseech her, "He is sorry for making a mistake." She would cruelly use our tears against us, demanding, "Give me a good reason to forgive him for his sins!" In the meantime, the boy, standing on tiptoes to lessen the impact of her upwards tugging, would pray that she would heed our prayers for his forgiveness.

Sister Saint Luke was unlikely to have actually strangled one of her charges, as the Arcadia Street Police Station was a mere five-minute walk from the school. Surely, if she killed a child, the paddy wagon would come and take her away. However, a fashion-forward student one day inadvertently thwarted her upwards tie-tugging maneuver, resulting in Sister Saint Luke's own humiliation in front of a class of little children.

That day came when Dennis Malloy was Sister's latest victim. He was pulled and prodded to a spot under the dangling light fixture. Once Sister had the attention of the fearful class, she grabbed Dennis by the tie, which came off in her hand. Dennis's mother, tired of the struggle with her multiple sons' morning Windsor knots, had purchased the newly available clip-on ties. Unbeknownst to Sister Saint Luke, Dennis could not be hoisted by his neckwear. Stunned by her loss of power over him, the class burst into horrified laughter. Sister turned with a mighty roar, grabbed her black leather book bag, and ran from the room. Oh no! We'd been through this scenario before!

Sister Saint Luke, when enraged (a daily event in Room 1A), would threaten to leave forever, telling her little students that she could not bear our sinful behavior. She routinely would shout at the class that she was never coming back, as she ran from the room. Tearfully, the fearful pupils would beg her to stay. When she finally had achieved mass hysteria, she would exit dramatically and leave us unattended and distraught. We didn't know what to do. Further, we had no clue that that petite woman was safely hidden between the open classroom door and the hallway wall.

After what seemed like hours, the nun from Room 1B would come into our classroom and remind us that it was our treacherous behavior that had devastated Sister Saint Luke. She would string us along, telling us that she had no idea where our teacher had gone. Sister Saint Luke's sidekick would harangue us till every child in the room was weeping profusely. She told us that by now, Sister Saint Luke was probably so far away that she would never come back. By then we were pitifully pleading for Sister Saint Luke's return. Finally, Sister Saint Luke would return to the classroom, tell us all what heathens we had been, and grudgingly agree to give us one more chance.

As if nothing at all had occurred, her co-conspirator would return to Class 1B. Returning to the front of the room, hoisting her heavy book bag while the sobs subsided, Sister Saint Luke would then smooth her starched wimple and put the pitch pipe to her lips for music lessons to commence. "Now, class. . . . " she'd begin.

Ironically, although I loved Saint Ambrose School, despite Sister's meanness, the only trauma I ever experienced in my five years in the school came from my first-grade classmates. It was a matter of my name, Judith. Many first-graders are in the process of losing baby teeth and thus speak with a temporary lisp. We had learned in our religion classes that Judas Iscariot, one of Jesus's Twelve Apostles, had betrayed his master to the authorities. Because Judas identified Jesus to the religious authorities in the Garden of Gethsemane, where Jesus was praying, Jesus was crucified and died. The betrayal of Christ in exchange for 30 pieces of silver by Judas was an oft-repeated lesson. Each time Sister called my name—Judith—my lisping fellow classmates heard "Judas." In horror, they would turn to me accusing, "Judas, you killed Jesus!"

I was humiliated again and again. I knew that I hadn't killed anyone, much less Jesus. Besides, I had no silver coins. It couldn't have been me, but everyone else seemed to think so. I was crushed by the renunciation I received each day from my classmates. All I wanted for Christmas was *their* two front teeth, so they could say not "Merry Christmas," but "Judith"!

Overall, my memories of my years at Saint Ambrose are overwhelmingly positive, but it seems on close reflection that I may have glossed over a number of events that made distinct impressions on me. And then there were whole academic years that left me with just fragments of memories, neither strongly negative nor positive. For instance, my second-grade teacher, Sister Angela, made very little impact on me. I recall only that she was a tall, slender young nun whose actual humanness was proven by the strands of pale blond hair that escaped her veil, gently framing her face. Aha! This was evidence contrary to our childhood belief that nuns were not real people.

Sister Angela had the responsibility of taking us through preparation for First Confession and First Holy Communion. The two Sacraments were highly anticipated in the life of young Catholics (especially the girls: For our First Communion, we got to wear a beautiful white dress and veil of our own). My parents even permitted me to get the white First Communion pocketbook sold by the school. It contained a Missal, a scapular (a devotional accessory worn under garments as a sign of piety), a set of Rosary beads, and a small plastic likeness of the infant Jesus. The extravagant allowance made by my parents in letting me get the optional religious accessories served to magnify how special the actual event was to be.

My memories of the year are completely involved with practicing confessing our sins, learning the Act of Contrition, and endless repetition of the rules and procedures for receiving Communion for the first time. At home we would flatten sliced white bread, and then cut out a disc using the rim of a jelly glass. These were our pretend Communion wafers, and we would practice the act of receiving the Sacrament for hours.

My only other memory of second grade was that I always won the spelling bees. Sister Angela once was so impressed that I could spell "Cape Canaveral" without being taught, that she gifted me with a brand-new toy that she had in the bottom drawer of her desk. Unusually, I was the object of both envy and admiration. I basked in the attention until I got home. My mother put a quick stop to my sin of expressing pride! Third grade was somewhat traumatic because of a second unpleasant nun whose focus seemed to be on picking on me alone. I once reluctantly begged my mother to please buy me a package of canceled stamps. Our family had little disposable income, and she knew I wouldn't have asked for the stamps if I hadn't been desperate. I was having increasing stomach aches in class when Sister Beatrice was present. For unknown reasons, she seemed to detest me. But what she loved were canceled stamps. Thoroughly embarrassed by my feelings of weakness, I even explained the situation to my mother. To my surprise, she bought me the stamps.

Anyone who brought in an envelope with a canceled stamp received a piece of candy from Sister's stash in the bottom drawer of her desk along with a smile from her craggy face. When I brought in the occasional stamp, however, I got a gumdrop and a nasty look. Clearly, I had not yet endeared myself to her. When I spotted the package of exotic canceled stamps at the post office, I thought it might be my one chance for a sign of approval from the testy teacher. I went to school happily clasping them. I tremulously walked up to Sister's desk and said, "I have stamps for you." She took them, snarled at the envelope filled with a variety of colorful canceled stamps, snatched it from my hand, and reached into the drawer and took out a chocolate. She thrust the candy at me so I would eat it before it melted in her hand.

I felt sick to my stomach, and not from the candy. She hadn't liked the stamps. She still didn't like me, and I had asked my mother for some of our limited household money for what amounted to a failed bribe. I went back to my seat ashamed and prayed for fourth grade to come quickly.

I thought I was the luckiest kid alive when I did get to fourth grade and was assigned to Mrs. Dyson, one of the few lay teachers in the school. A dramatic event occurred with my placement in her class. I was, for the only time in my life, teacher's pet. But with good luck comes obligation and I was torn by decision-making that I struggled with for the school year. Putting it more simply, as pet, I was put in charge when Mrs. Dyson was out of the classroom for a coffee or lavatory break. I was to sit at her desk and keep an eye on my classmates for forbidden behavior such as talking or horseplay. I was then to report to Mrs. Dyson on return from her break.

What a dilemma. I didn't want to mislead Mrs. Dyson but I didn't want to betray my friends and classmates. I did the only thing that I could do. I kept my eyes closed the entire time I was sitting in the front of the classroom, opening them only when I heard her cheery voice on return. "Judith, how did everyone behave?" I could truthfully answer, "I didn't see anything." My classmates snickered, and Mrs. Dyson smiled with satisfaction. I breathed a sigh of relief . . . every single school day.

The other task which might have seemed an obligation to other students that was a pleasure to me was the responsibility for doing the copying every morning. I was sent to the office, papers in hand, to happily use the mimeograph, or ditto machine, depending on which was available in the school. Both early types of copiers used a master copy that would be "run off" by the operator (me). Both types of copiers also gave off a tantalizing smell, to those of us who found the scent to be intoxicating. As teacher's pet, I made all of Mrs. Dyson's copies every morning, and always came back to the downstairs classroom with a smile.

It was hard work being teacher's pet, but I loved it! And I never had to buy her anything. She had my lifelong devotion for her kindness toward me.

That experience flip-flopped the next school year when I became the object of my teacher's wrath! In the fifth grade at Saint Ambrose School, the task of perfectly mastering the Palmer Method of cursive handwriting was a primary objective. Sister Mary Paulette, my teacher, had the most beautiful script, and appointed herself the Palmer Master. She designated it her own personal responsibility to assure that all of *her* students made it through fifth grade with handwriting that was indistinguishable from her own. We were meant to be identifiable by our handwriting as one of Sister Mary Paulette's successes.

According to Sister Paulette, the Palmer rules required that one write with the wrist totally flat on the writing surface. Instead, my hand always curled like a claw as I gripped my writing implements. I still managed to write, but not to the satisfaction of Sister. The entire class had Palmer lessons every day until we were able to duplicate her perfect written alphabet, both upper and lower case. As each child was unofficially certified as performing the assigned task, they were allowed to leave the classroom for recess.

I stopped getting recess at all, as she scolded me for the way I held my hand to write. She tried to balance a penny flat on the back of my wrist to remind me of the correct writing position. The penny promptly rolled to the floor as I practiced my letters. Sister began to keep those of us who had difficulty with the Palmer method after school for remedial penmanship lessons. Each school day, more of the stay-after kids got released when they were successful at writing the way she demanded of us. But I just couldn't write with a flat wrist. Sister got frustrated and put a heavy book on the back of my forearm to hold it still. The book fell to the floor with a thud as my wrist turned thumb upwards. In a fury, Sister Paulette grabbed a ruler and struck me about eight times in rapid succession. I pulled my hand away, muttering to myself, "That will help me. A broken wrist!" She kicked me out of the classroom, yelling to my back, "You write like a Chinaman and you always will!"

Following protocol, I did not tell my parents, as I would be punished at home for upsetting a teacher. But Sister had branded me a Palmer drop-out, her first. It didn't matter to her that I was first-row, first seat in all of my academic and religious studies.

Oh, Sister Mary Paulette, it would have been much more Christ-like to be kind to those of us who were Palmer-impaired!

I clearly value my parochial school education: Many years later, I sent my own three daughters to Catholic elementary and high school. Despite the harsh disciplinary measures and their lack of clear guidance regarding philosophies of education of young children, the Catholic nuns of my day provided a sound foundation for self-discipline and an appreciation for the value of learning.

8

The Triple-Deckers of Dorchester

The multi-family dwellings many called "triple-deckers" had been built so that the children of immigrants who had migrated to Boston for work could live comfortably. The houses had wooden stairs inside and out, vast landings on each floor, and carved wooden bannisters, commonly constructed of gleaming mahogany. The apartments contained built-in china cabinets, pocket doors, and pristine hardwood floors which would later, as a sign of the prosperity of the tenants, be covered with wall-to-wall carpeting. The houses had both front and back porches. If screened in, the back porches were often called "piazzas." But by the time we lived in them, the porches, other than the ones on the first floor, were usually too decrepit for us to use. Instead, they hung like droopy diapers from the buildings themselves.

But not at 54 Parkman Street. Our third-floor back porch on Parkman was well maintained although a faulty window lock enabled our cat to push against the glass and pop open the window. We loved to sit out there, with or without the ingenious cat, because of our unobstructed view of the weather beacon that had been affixed in 1950 to the original John Hancock Building. The beacon flashed a sequence of weather-predicting colors, which, for Boston residents, obviated the need to listen to meteorologists'

53

forecasts. Most of those who live in or grew up in or around Boston are familiar with the rhyme that translated the meaning of the flashing colors:

Steady Blue, clear view
Flashing Blue, clouds due
Steady Red, storms ahead
Flashing red, snow instead.

The standard three-family homes, or triple-deckers, typically had a single main front door that entered generous hallway spaces with stairs extending up to the third floor. To actually get inside each apartment, one had to go through another locked door from the hallway. All the years I lived in them, the front halls were a safe haven for us kids, especially in inclement weather. We had the run of the halls, up and down the stairs, but were safe from the streets—and perceived ourselves to be free of parental eyes. Yet we could easily go in and out of our own apartments as desired.

Triple-decker housing was ideal for the narrow residential lots in Dorchester. As well, it was economical for builders to stack identical units on one foundation and under one roof. The apartments were much more spacious than people imagined. Our Parkman Street apartment was on the third floor of a standard triple-decker. However, the railroad-car floorplan had all rooms running off a center hall, a long slender corridor. The kitchens typically were at the end of the corridor at the back of the house. Off the kitchen was a good-sized pantry. A large living space suitable for entertaining would be just inside the front door. Spaces designed for dining rooms were very often converted into bedrooms instead, to accommodate the large working-class families occupying each floor. Tall and wide exterior windows, and inside window transoms, provided natural light and an airy feeling to the living spaces, in contrast to tenement living. As well, bay windows on the fronts of the houses made them look even broader. Views of the city skyline were visible from many residents' front or back porches, and a very easy commute made neighborhoods like Dorchester function as "streetcar suburbs" of the city of Boston.

Each three-family house also had a spacious cellar, where the furnace, the pile of coal for heat, and the majority of storage space for the apartments were located. Some of the few shortcomings of the triple-deckers were their tiny yards, the buildings being very close to each other, and extremely limited parking. However, in the 1950s and 1960s, families most often had one car, if any, per family. Nearly everything we needed was in walking distance. But then again, "walking distance" in those days could be anything up to three miles or so—each way.

Our lifestyles were likely to have been healthier then compared to the decades in which fast food restaurants became ubiquitous. There was scant need for gym memberships for exercise, and cars were rarely used to ferry us around the corner for some grocery shopping. However, I must acknowledge that our home-cooked foods were often fried in lard (pure animal fat), cigarette smoking was a far less expensive habit than it is now and significantly more prevalent, and many health maintenance and disease prevention strategies had not yet improved life expectancies. So, the tendency to romanticize the past as an ideally healthy way of living must be carefully examined and reframed. That being said, I loved my Dorchester childhood and nearly everything about it, especially the Saturday morning crispy fried dough cooked in sizzling hot Goodhue's animal fat.

My parents kept our Dorchester homes in pristine condition, often buying a somewhat rundown three-family and totally restoring and modernizing it. They purchased their initial home on Edwin Street when I was ten years old. That was their first property; they had free rein to pull apart decaying elements and restore them, commanding higher rents with each new "old" home that they transformed.

We kids, at young ages, became near-experts at peeling off layers and layers of old wallpaper, and sanding down worn and flaking paint prior to re-staining or repainting. Kitchens were retrofitted with modern washing machines and, on occasion, dryers. By the 1970s, dishwashers were becoming more common inside the apartments. As history has demonstrated, these modern conveniences which were predicted to provide more time for the harried housewife simply gave her more time to take on more jobs both inside and outside of the family home, and also within the paid workforce.

I cannot say that I loved any one of our three family houses in Dorchester more than another, but it was definitely a close tie between our Parkman Street dwelling and our Edwin Street home. The difference was that we owned the home on Edwin Street, and my mother didn't need to be nervous about a stern and unfriendly landlady who demanded her rent exactly on the first of each month. Although my parents were both very judicious with money, my mother's sensitivity made her dread the knock on the door with the imperious demand for the monthly fee for occupancy which was never even a day behind. When my parents finally became land-lords, it was more their style to wait for the tenants to bring down the rent, and to forgive the occasional lateness, as they had been in the same precarious position as tenants-at-will. Their generosity of spirit was noted by their apartment occupants, and, unbeknownst to them, by their children as well.

9

⌘

Neighborhood Life in Dorchester: Privacy, Pilfering, and Table Talk Pie

We had a street full of friends on Parkman Street: Bugsy, the Greeley family, the Abbotts, and numerous others. We particularly liked Mr. Charles Abbott, the only adult that encouraged us to call him by his nickname, "Chuck." I thought him particularly attentive because he would listen to me singing on the sidewalk in between our houses. He often asked me if I could sing, "Far, Far, Away." I was thrilled at the request but stymied because I didn't know the song in question. I finally figured out that he was asking me to sing *at a considerable distance from our homes*.

Our friend Bugsy lived in the corner house on our side of the street. She was called "Bugsy" because of her frequent cases of head lice. No one seemed particularly bothered by the contagiousness of head lice at the time, and the name was given to her by another kid who noticed that she was always scratching her head.

Bugsy was also a good friend because of an interesting architectural element of her front porch. For some unknown reason, a two-by-four nailed from the porch upper railing perpendicular to the house served as a monkey bar of sorts for Bugsy, my younger sister Jeanie, and me. Often, while playing outside Bugsy's front door, the three of us would hang upside down by the backs of our knees from the parallel bar. I have no recall why we did that, except that it was there and so we hung while chatting, until my best friend Patrick came looking for me or we were called home for meals.

Directly across the street from us on the second floor of 49 Parkman Street lived the Donnelly family. Patrick was my best friend from the age of 6 until we were twelve. We played together well and at times found occasion to engage in mutually entertaining hooliganism. As I approached puberty, I found Patrick repulsive, but the event that triggered my discomfort happened much earlier.

Patrick was the oldest of four kids; following Patrick were Finn, Maeve, and later, baby Aisling, for whom I babysat—my first job. Our first episode of girl-boy dissonance happened when we were seven. The Kirwans and Donnellys, like most of our relatives and friends, had wardrobes greatly enriched by hand-me-downs from cousins and neighbors. Patrick Donnelly's father, however, out of a misguided sense of pride, would not accept hand-me-down clothing for his children. He directed his wife to outfit their children only in attire that they bought themselves. Thus, the Donnelly children wore their clothing until it no longer fit any of them or was truly threadbare. Thus it was that a broken trouser zipper resulted in my first gagging at the sight of Patrick's pasty white "private" flesh. On one rainy day, we were playing inside his family apartment and he went to use the bathroom. He soon called me in to help him. I was stunned. I had never been told not to, but it didn't seem right to go into a bathroom with a boy. I resisted, simply not answering Patrick's summons. He called out again, "Judy, come in here. I need your help!" My Romper Room ethic kicked in and I heeded Patrick's plea, despite my discomfort.

He had finished urinating (polite Catholic children never said "peeing") but he hadn't flushed yet, and that nauseated me. But what caught my attention even more starkly was the gaping front of his pants. In his hand was a large, opened safety pin. Apparently, his zipper was broken yet the pants still deemed wearable. Mrs. Donnelly had given him an extra diaper pin and showed him how to open and close the broken-zippered placket on the front of his drawers using the unwieldy diaper pin. But after doing his business, Patrick couldn't manage to hold both sides of the fabric closed with one hand while trying to fasten the oversized pin with his other hand. He handed me the pin and asked, "Will you please close me?" I blanched but was reluctant to ignore a friend in need. As I was eye level with the lower front of his body, I brandished the pin, hoping to avoid getting his white briefs caught up as I helped him recover his modesty. Instead, I was greeted by the sight of a shockingly pale boy's part inadvertently still exposed. I avoided him for weeks after, but finally got tired of just hanging from Bugsy's parallel bar and rejoined Patrick in play.

The second most memorable shared experience with Patrick was our revenge on Maroon, the local shopkeeper. Maroon owned the corner variety store on Patrick's side of the street. As children would do in those days, we earned money scouting for returnable tonic bottles and cashing them in at Maroon's. Each empty would net us two cents. After cashing in enough bottles, we could share a candy bar, honestly earned yet illicit according to family rules for being "between meals." Patrick and I trolled the gutters for empties, amassing enough within a half-hour to buy the candy. Maroon was not happy about taking the returnable bottles and would yell at us each time we brought in the results of our foraging: *"No more today! I have no room!"*

Patrick and I felt it was unfair of Maroon to put limits on our earnings, and resented his so freely raising his voice at us when we were clearly working, and when loud chastisement was something we felt only parents had the privilege of doing. After numerous maddening encounters, Patrick and I put our heads together. (In this instance, I was relieved *not* to be collecting bottles and hatching schemes with lice-afflicted Bugsy!) We came up with the following: If Maroon yelled at us publicly one more time, we would come in even *more* frequently with bottles to exchange for cash. We knew we could become more efficient in our collecting by purloining them from a readily available, unmonitored source: wooden cases filled with empties stacked in the Donnellys' alleyway just beyond the open rear door of Maroon's.

Maroon yelled. We stole. Boldly, we snatched bottles from out back, and returned them through the front door. Maroon was steaming at our increased yield. He reluctantly handed over our cash but yelled less and less. Had we gotten caught we would have been turned over to our parents for our theft. It never occurred to us that the punishment would likely have far outweighed the crime.

Admittedly it might have been justified for our first experiment in larceny, and also retribution. But, as we had silently concurred, our theft was justified by Maroon's explosive temper frequently directed our way. Ultimately, it was guilt, and not investigation by Maroon as to why his bottle supply remained steady despite an uptick in returns, that interrupted our scheme.

A Parkman Street neighbor much dearer to me than Maroon was Mrs. Dooley, the sweet lady who occupied the tiny third-floor apartment above the Donnellys'. 76-year-old Mrs. Dooley, a frail, diabetic woman, was attended to by her adult daughter each morning. The younger Dooley would arise early; wash, feed, and dress her mother; and situate her in an easy chair on the front porch of their home. The Dooley daughter then went off to work for a morning shift at a local business.

The old woman would sit by herself for hours, becoming lonely and hungry. As young as I was, I never gave a thought as to how she might be toileted for those long, solitary, four-hour stretches, but Mrs. Dooley was far more concerned with snack breaks than bathroom breaks.

Kids from large families who lived in Dorchester were woken early on non-school days, encouraged to consume the hot porridge or cold cereal prepared by Mom, make their beds, perform ablutions prior to and after breakfast, and then get out of the house and not come back until lunchtime. The routine was repeated at midday, and as we got older, afternoon activities and obligations were somewhat consistent with those of the mornings. An early supper was shared by the family, dishes washed, and the older kids were allowed to go back outside, if only to reduce the noise levels inside family homes.

So, my morning was fairly unstructured once I ran down the front hall steps from our spacious third-floor apartment. As I played in the street, alone or with siblings and neighborhood kids, Mrs. Dooley would often sweetly beseech me, "Judy. Judy? Would you please come over and help an old woman?" Of course, I would help her. Lack of family supervision for both of us provided a mutually satisfactory arrangement.

Because of her diabetes, Mrs. Dooley's intake of sweets was necessarily monitored by the adult daughter. However, while the cat's away, the mice will eat Table Talk Apple Pie on the front stoop.

After she called me to join her, and I complied, Mrs. Dooley would reach down inside her house-coated bosom and extract a knotted handkerchief. Struggling with her arthritic fingers, she would untie it, and pull out coins. Counting out exactly 59 cents, she'd hand them to me, and send me to Maroon's for a large Table Talk Apple Pie. The full-sized pastry was meant to provide a substantial dessert for a whole family. I'd bring back the eagerly awaited pie to where the old woman hungrily lusted. The fact that we had no plates, no utensils, or even a bit of a napkin, did not stand in the way of our feast.

Mrs. Dooley would send me into the tiny, fenced-in front yard to find a stick. She said it was best after the rain, because "loose dirt" would have been washed off the branch or random shard of wood, which would be used to cut the luscious pie. Mrs. Dooley eagerly tore open the box, leaving the pie in its tin. She would take the stick from me and cut into the dessert unevenly, thrusting a piece of apple pastry directly into my cupped palms. She would eat from the tin, breaking off pieces of the pie and bringing it to her mouth which she opened like a hungry bird, then close her eyes in deep satisfaction as she enjoyed the forbidden treat. We would eat, and eat, until we were beyond sated. Cleanup would be with wet leaves, also gathered from the little front yard, to wipe our sticky faces and hands. Mrs. Dooley would then direct me around to the backyard to the garbage pails, where I was instructed to hide all the detritus of our tasty misadventure.

As with my sneaky dealings with Patrick Donnelly and the stolen tonic bottles, Mrs. Dooley and I never got caught. However, you might say we were never openly *confronted* about our chicanery. I am quite certain that Mrs. Dooley's otherwise unexplained rises in blood sugar levels, as checked by the daughter returned from work, evoked questions from her doctor. It is hard to imagine how my diminished desire for second portions of supper at home could have gone unnoticed either. Yet it did. My mother did raise her eyebrows and glance in my direction when I didn't automatically reach for more mashed potatoes. However, the most likely sign that an illicit sweet was being enjoyed by Mrs. Dooley and me in our unsupervised late mornings was our refusal of dessert after the main meal of the day. Hours later, we were both still burping from our luscious large portions of Table Talk Apple Pie.

10

Kathy's New Bike

As the oldest child in the family, when Kathy advanced from a tricycle to a two-wheeler, our parents gave her a brand-new blue "grown-up" bike. Kathy easily maneuvered the two-wheeler, riding it up and down Parkman Street endlessly. I admired the bike and admit to having been envious, but Kathy did share. When the bike was still brand-new, and she was at her Girl Scout meeting in the Protestant church halfway up the block from our apartment she graciously let me borrow it for the duration of the meeting.

I timed my privilege by listening for the opening recitation of the Girl Scout Promise. I silently mouthed, along with Kathy's troop, every word, "On my honor, I will try to serve God and my country, to help other people at all times, and to live by the Girl Scout law." As I mounted the borrowed bike, I knew the girls would be holding up their three middle fingers of their right hand, making the Girl Scout Sign. Songs and traditional Girl Scout activities would follow. I was now on a borrowed bike on borrowed time. I monitored the progress of the meeting intermittently through the church's open windows while I attempted to master the two-wheeler in the 55 minutes left until dismissal.

I was absolutely enamored of that magnificent set of wheels, and determined that I, too, would learn to ride it on that very day. I was quickly able to ride up and down the street independently. I couldn't wait to show Kathy and the rest of our family that I had taught myself to ride the bike unassisted. But I was disappointed knowing that Kathy expected it back after her meeting, and I would have limited time to demonstrate my mastery. The clock ticked down until the meeting approached the end, with the Girl Scout Pledge. I headed back to the church, anticipating the ending song sung in unison, "Day is done, gone the sun from the lakes, from the hills, from the sky. All is well, safely rest, God is nigh." As I proudly rode the bike back to the meeting site, the bike chain suddenly fell off! My terror that Kathy would kill me for breaking her new bike was mixed with grave disappointment I could not show off my new skill. Kathy came out, yelled at me, and grabbed the bike to walk it home. I trudged miserably down Parkman Street, awaiting a punishment that never came. After supper, my father merely replaced the broken chain. I was never allowed use of the bike again. When I was old enough to join Girl Scouts myself, I walked to meetings and back home.

Kathy rode the bike all over our section of Dorchester. One afternoon, she went off with her best friend Joyce to Orbit's Department Store, off Victory Road. About an hour later, she arrived home crying hysterically. She had left her precious bike parked outside the store but returned to find it gone. She and Joyce searched the parking lot, but alas, no bike was to be found. They sought out the store manager, who coldly said, "You leave new bikes outside, they get stolen." It turned out that Kathy's loss was mine as well. Now that I could ride a two-wheeler, I begged my parents for my own. They grimly said that they could not replace Kathy's bike with a new bike. She would have to use a bike passed down by an older cousin. Nothing was said about whether I would ever see a bike of my own.

But not so long afterward, as I walked home from school, Jeanie and I stopped at the corner to wait for the traffic lights to signal that we could cross safely. As the lights changed, our father coincidentally stopped the car at that same intersection. Even though we crossed right in front of the family car, he seemed not to notice us. I must have been imagining it but there appeared to be a navy-blue bike squished into the back seat of the Nash. In fact, he had stopped at a secondhand store on the way home from work and had chosen a gently used bike for me.

My father, as industrious as ever, refurbished the bike for me.

I accepted the secondhand bike with silent chagrin. I quickly grew to love it, though, riding from one end of Dorchester to the other. I was born to ride this very bike, I thought! Jeanie now joined me on my travels. Coming back home after an afternoon's outing, we again stopped at the same traffic signal to go home to Parkman Street, this time with me straddling my now much-loved bike. Two boys, not much older than we were, approached us belligerently. One sneered at me, "You have my old bike!" I immediately denied the charge: "No, this is my new bike. I got it for my birthday." He laughed meanly and said, "It's a boy's bike. It has a crossbar. It was my old one and you got it from the Morgie." It was humiliating to be caught owning a secondhand bicycle. The "Morgie" was Morgan Memorial Industries, a long-standing non-profit that sold used goods at multiple locations. Again, I denied the boy's assertions, and blushed furiously, wishing the crossing signal to turn green so we could escape his mental cruelty.

No luck. He had the time to lean forward, saying, "I can prove it to you. *My* bike was blue." He scraped paint off the crossbar with his fingernails, peeling away the red paint and exposing the original navy base color. Having thoroughly shamed me, the callous boys laughed, and left the scene of my mortification. However, I thought about the effort my father had put into providing me with a much-wanted two-wheeler of my own. He had taken the time to find me a bike that wouldn't attract a thief as Kathy's shiny new bike had. He had cleaned the bike, scraped its old, peeling blue paint, and sprayed it a bright red in an effort to provide me with my birthday bike, a bike new *to me*.

While this was a valuable life-lesson, I still imagine smacking that smug kid's face. I am willing to bet that he has spent the rest of his life kicking puppies.

As for me, I proudly rode my red bike throughout Dorchester until we moved to South Weymouth. When I turned 16, unbeknownst to my parents, I journeyed miles on my trusty bike to the Registry of Motor Vehicles in Quincy to apply for my learner's permit. I got my license and bought my own car. It was the Marina blue 1967 Chevy II my mother had allowed me to select from the glossy brochure when she and my father purchased it two years earlier. They decided to replace the Chevy II with a larger family-friendly red Ford Pinto station wagon. But rather than trade the car in at the dealership as a down payment on the Pinto, they allowed me to buy it for myself.

Take that, my torturer! Years later when I was tooling around Weymouth in my little deuce coupe, I consoled myself with the likelihood that the mean boy had probably only advanced to hitch-hiking! If I ever saw him thumbing on the side of the road, I would lean out the window and yell, "Hey kid, I graduated from your used bike to my used car. Where are your new wheels now?!"

11

⁓

Fire!

Just my title alone makes me shudder a bit. Is there anyone who isn't terrified by fire? Is there anyone who doesn't have nightmares about fire? Is there anyone whose lives have been untouched by fire?

The Cocoanut Grove fire is one of the deadliest fires ever to have struck Boston. The initial death count was 492. Untold numbers of victims suffered burns, infections, respiratory disorders, and other acute or chronic problems, and died hours to years after the fire itself, never tallied in the tolls of lives taken by the Cocoanut Grove fire.

The Cocoanut Grove was a popular nightclub in the Park Square section of Boston. The address was listed as Piedmont Street, although the rambling structure was not confined to one building or single level.

At approximately 10:15 p.m. on November 28, 1942, one of the deadliest structure fires in the history of the United States had begun in Cocoanut Grove's Melody Lounge, a basement room of the nightclub. The extremely high death count was due, in part, to many violations of the fire codes in existence at that time, but the initial death count exceeded even the building's official capacity.

Although the nightclub was significantly overcrowded when the conflagration occurred, many more people had been expected to be in attendance. Because of the prowess of Boston College's football players during the 1942 season, a Boston College victory against rival Holy Cross College that night had been assumed, and a celebration party at the Cocoanut Grove planned. When Holy Cross prevailed on the football field, the Boston College celebration party scheduled for the Grove was canceled. Even so, because it was Thanksgiving weekend and many wartime servicemen and women were in Boston, the club allowed more than 1,000 revelers to cram into the space meant to accommodate a maximum of 460.

Few people in Massachusetts were unconnected to people, places, or situations associated with the deadly blaze. That is true for my family as well. My mother, Jean Currivan Kirwan, was first cousin to Don Currivan, a Boston College football star. When Holy Cross unexpectedly won the big game, most BC players opted out of the victory party at the Grove. Don Currivan's life and that of many of his teammates were saved by that decision.

Our second family connection to the Cocoanut Grove fire involved my paternal grandfather, Thomas Michael Kirwan, of Boston Police Department's Mounted Division who was called to duty as a first responder at the noted club on the night of the disaster. My grandfather achieved a brief period of local fame as he was featured in the December 7, 1942 issue of *Life Magazine*, an enormously popular national publication, as a rescuer carrying out a fire victim from Cocoanut Grove.

This, however, was not as personally agonizing an event to our entire family as the Boston fire which took the life of Pa Kirwan's daughter, my paternal aunt Rosalie Kirwan Griffin, on December 28, 1960. The *Boston Globe* article chronicling her death says that 37-year-old Aunt Rosalie, a former Marine, had been working recently as a clerk for the Massachusetts State House. She lived just blocks away, alone, on the third floor of a four-story structure at 73 Mount Vernon Street. The conflagration began in the apartment above hers; Aunt Rosalie apparently became blinded by smoke and stepped out a window which she believed led to a fire escape. There was such a window, but in her confusion, my aunt stepped out of the window to the side of the one with the fire escape. She plunged 60 feet to her death, landing on a patio below. She was found by first responders and taken by ambulance to Massachusetts General Hospital but died en route.

In adulthood, I told my mother that I remembered when someone came to our apartment on the night of Aunt Rosalie's death, summoning my father. My mother answered, "You were six years old. You couldn't possibly remember that." I recalled to her that we had been eating supper, my father having arrived home from work no more than a half-hour previous to the knock on our third-floor Parkman Street door. I had to answer the front door, but my father got there ahead of me. He opened it to a man standing somberly, waiting to deliver news to my father. Dad had removed his work shirt prior to supper and stood at the front door in an undershirt, and without shoes on. I was embarrassed for my father, doing what I perceived as receiving an unexpected guest dressed in this sloppy way. My father gruffly told me to go back to the kitchen. My father briefly heard what the unfamiliar man had to say to him, hurried back into the house, finished dressing, threw on an overcoat and left.

I knew that my father never left the house once he had come home from work for the night other than the rare occasions when he and my mother went to see an early movie. Thus, when I related to my mother my recall of the stranger at our door, she acknowledged that I couldn't have remembered all of those details if I had not witnessed my father being summoned to identify his sister's body.

In May of the same year, seven months prior to the fire that killed Aunt Rosalie, an accidental, non-fatal fire in our Parkman Street neighborhood deeply touched all our families. The victim in this fire, just a few houses up from ours at 42 Parkman, was Richard Gottlich, age 16. Richard survived the explosion in his basement workroom caused by a chemical blast. Richie was an honor student at Matignon High School in Cambridge. On May 22, 1960, Mr. and Mrs. Gottlich were at a parent-teacher meeting, Richie's older sister Janice was working as a nurse at Carney Hospital, and his younger sister Karen, a friend of my sister Kathy, was in her bedroom.

Richie was in the family basement at 9:30 p.m., when the chemicals he had been working with suddenly exploded in his hands. Neighbors rushed into his smoke-filled home after the loud blast that shook their wooden duplex. They found Richie prostrate near his workbench, bleeding profusely. An occupant of the adjoining apartment ran into a second-floor bedroom and carried Richie's younger sister Karen to safety. Richie was brought to

Carney Hospital after suffering second-degree burns on his face, hands, chest, and stomach. He was placed on the danger list, but he survived. Four firefighters suffered smoke inhalation from the thick chemical fumes. Richie lived to talk about the fire, but all of the families in the neighborhood were badly shaken.

I remember seeing the first responders from my third-floor bedroom window arriving at his house. Some time after Richie's accident, I had my first fire nightmare that I can clearly recall. In my dream, I was sitting at my bedroom window, just as I had done the night of Richie's accident, but with my nose pressed against the screen. In my dream, a fireman extended a ladder and climbed all the way up to my window. He lit a match and held the flame to my nose through the screen. I didn't pull away. I allowed my skin to burn. I felt no fright in the dream, although I still remember it clearly. The fires left me with a lifelong terror of dying in a fire.

About Edith and Thomas Kirwan and their family of ten kids, there are still legends and lore that have been passed on to children, grandchildren, and great grandchildren. My Aunt Pat was considered the unofficial family historian for most of her life. I started to assume the mantle at a fairly young age, because I was always so fascinated by what she would tell about family occurrences involving nearly every member of our extensive Kirwan family. For years I have been referred to as "the Aunt Pat of the family." Recently, I had the pleasure of speaking with someone who recognized the Kirwan name, which I consider an essential part of who I am. She asked me, "Are you a Kirwan from the Kirwan family that lived on Hopestill Street?" I was shocked. The last Kirwans left Hopestill Street in the late 1970s. I answered in the affirmative. She told me that she clearly remembered my grandfather, the Boston cop, and my grandmother. She remarked on the fact that there were so many kids (although that was not at all unusual for a Boston Irish family).

She then told me that the incident that she remembered the most vividly was seeing a few of the kids surfing on a still-flaming mattress that was being carried out of the front door of 5 Hopestill Street by the two older boys. This was a new fire memory even to me! She said, "I couldn't even imagine! It was on fire, there were a few kids sitting in the middle of the fire, as the big boys ran and dumped the whole mess, including the younger siblings, in the front yard. They were all laughing hysterically, and your grandmother was hollering at them out from the porch." I was grateful for her recall and thought that it was a relief to hear of a non-injurious fire story in which everyone escaped unharmed. Through tragedies, triumphs, tribulations, and treasured moments, our oral and written histories keep family memories alive.

12

⚹

The Aptly Named Sister Miseria of Saint Mark's

After I completed fifth grade at Saint Ambrose School, my family moved from Parkman to Edwin Street. Kathy was about to enter eighth grade at Saint Ambrose and did not change schools, despite her new, longer walk, since it allowed her to graduate with her classmates at the end of the 1966 school year. Lonnie and I transferred to Saint Mark's but there were no openings for Jeanie, so she stayed at Saint Ambrose with Kathy.

I was assigned to Sister Miseria's sixth grade class at Saint Mark's. I was delighted because my new next-door neighbor Joanie was in my class. When his family moved as well, Patrick Donnelly was transferred to Saint Mark's the same year. However, sixth-grade boys were considered creepy by many sixth-grade girls, myself included, so Patrick played a much-diminished role in my life at Saint Mark's. I clung to Joanie to help me to adjust to this mean new teacher, but no matter how much Joanie tried to intervene, Sister Miseria made it crystal-clear that she did not like me. In fact, she only liked a couple of students out of our whole class, so I should not have taken her rudeness personally.

I had always been a strong student. I earned all As at Saint Mark's. That was problematic: I was displacing Sister's favorite, Marcia McLennan. Marcia's hallowed role was "smartest girl in the class." Each time I earned a better grade, Sister Miseria would insult me. I caught on fairly quickly, especially once other students started telling me, "Sister Miseria hates you. You do better than Marcia does."

I got my dander up and determined I would not fake a poor performance in school just to please Sister or her pet student. We changed classes for math and science, and my grades in those subjects were also consistently higher than Marcia's. Sister Miseria was furious. One day Sister insulted me in front of the class, saying to me outright, "Marcia McLennan is the smartest girl in the school!" The smartest thing about me was my mouth, however, and I retorted without thinking, "Anything Marcia can do, I can do better." Sister, Marcia McLennan, and Marcia's friends were highly offended, and responded with intense dislike toward me. The bitter nun looked at me and retorted, "I hate your long hair!"

I was losing this battle that I faced every single day. I asked my mother to let me have my long hair cut that afternoon. My mother was aware of the struggle I was enduring at Saint Mark's, but she also did not like my long, straight hair. She allowed me to have it cut short and styled at the local beauty parlor. The stylist shaped my blond hair into a cute cut, leaving long strands in front with which I could make pin curls. I went to school the next day to face Sister Miseria. Joanie tried to ingratiate me with Sister by asking, "Sister, do you like Judy's hair cut? It's not long anymore!" Sister looked me over and then snorted, "What are those ugly fishhooks in front?"

I was far from the only one being picked on by the teacher. Each day after recess, Sister would place her rotund body in the middle of the classroom doorway. As her form occupied half of the width of the door frame, students had to squeeze sideways through to avoid letting their bodies touch hers. This odd woman was not trying to make physical contact with us in any way. She was actually smelling each and every one of us as we passed by her. Sister would take a good sniff as both girls and boys entered the classroom, making a nasty remark to most about failures in personal hygiene: "Your socks smell. Wash them before you come back to school." "Do you know the meaning of halitosis? You have bad breath. Get some mouthwash and use it!" "Did you ever hear of deodorant? Get some to get rid of your body odor!" The worst of all was "Somebody didn't change their underwear this morning.

You stink!" Sister's meanness increased as the year passed, with her finally getting angry even at Marcia McLennan. When that happened, Marcia and I bonded and stayed friends for the last few years that I lived in Dorchester.

Emboldened, I began to engage other kids in mischievous acts related to the convent. The worst we did was no more than irksome. Our petty misbehaviors entertained us and that made us feel less powerless against Sister's not so subtle torture. The first game I convinced other dissatisfied classmates to play was "ring and run." We did just what it sounds like. We would ring the convent bell shrilly and then hide. The poor old nuns would make their way down the long hallways of the convent in their orthopedic shoes just to find that there was no one there. We only did that a few times before we felt badly for our misplaced aggression. Unfortunately, we had no way to indicate to the frail older nuns who stayed on as housekeepers or cooks in exchange for their keep that they were not our targets. But I had to keep my sanity intact by committing minor acts of deviance in retaliation for Sister Miseria's cruelty.

And yet we got a bit more personal. The nun's clothesline of baggy white bloomers and cotton undershirts hung behind a large hedge in back of the convent. Initially, we would just run through and yank off the clothespins so the undergarments landed in a heap on the ground, needing to be rewashed before *they* were wearing stinky underwear. As the year went on, and Sister Miseria got no nicer, I got a new idea that totally flummoxed the Sisters. I snuck into other laundry-bearing backyards, making off with a pair or two of men's undershorts. I didn't want them for myself! I swapped them out for nun's undies on the convent clothesline. I didn't even try to engage co-conspirators in this prank, because I couldn't count on someone not developing a case of loose lips and ratting me out to the principal.

Either I never got caught or Sister Miseria realized that I was behind the tomfoolery and became frightened of what I might do next. She became slightly nicer to me in the classroom. But she had an ulterior motive. One morning, in a sickeningly sweet voice, she asked me to come up to the front of the classroom. I did as she asked, and she told me she was going to enter my work in the Archdiocesan Safety Poster contest. Perplexed, I said, "But I'm not good at art! And I haven't done a poster."

Sister gave me a saccharine smile and said, "We'll work on the project together." Now I was suspicious. Why would she have me enter a contest that I would surely lose? Sister asked me to stay after school for the next five days. As it was still only November, I wanted to keep a fairly low profile. Since I walked home from school, I simply needed to inform my mother that I would be late each day working on a project with Sister. As surprised as I was, my mother accepted at face value the change in Sister's attitude toward me and granted permission for me to be late coming home from school.

The first afternoon I met with Sister, she told me the poster contest rules. I was to use only four colors, cut out a design for the artwork, and glue pre-cut letters to form an appropriate slogan. "Yes, Sister," I answered, afraid of how badly this could go. Unexpectedly however, Sister Miseria handed me a white poster board, a beautifully cut out black owl, a yellow paper umbrella, yellow feet for the owl, and prepared green letters for the slogan which she had already composed. Sister told me to just glue each piece in places that corresponded with her tracings, or "preparation" as she called it. The handful of what seemed to be random letters would, when finished, read, "Be Wise. Be Alert in Bad Weather." All the criteria for the contest were met without any effort on my part besides gluing cut paper exactly as she had directed me.

That only took a couple of afternoons. Then Sister had me sign my name and class number on the back of the poster. I was befuddled. Did she really want me to take credit for work that wasn't my own? But Sister said that I should do it, so I did. When it was completed, Sister wore an expression I did not recognize: She was smiling at me. It turned out that she happened to be an artist—and a con artist. The poster contest was not open to teachers, but she had been determined to win, and she accomplished her objective using me.

Not surprisingly, the poster *did* win First Place in the Archdiocesan Safety contest. I was invited with my parents to another church in the Archdiocese where the winning work would be displayed. My parents were invited. I was honestly so confused that I didn't recognize Sister's cheating. I went to the poster presentation with my mother and father, got up when my name was called as first-place winner, and received a prize envelope. Before I even had a chance to look at the envelope, Sister loudly announced, "And Judith has offered to donate her winnings to the orphanages." I knew that I had been snookered by a sister. I downplayed the whole incident to my parents, and we never spoke of it again.

A couple of months later there was another contest: the Archdiocesan Poetry contest. I didn't like poetry. I was not going to enter on my own, and I was not playing along this time with Sister Miseria. No one in the class would willingly participate in a poetry contest, so Sister got the better of us by requiring an original poem about Christmas as homework.

In my house, as soon as we got home from school, we could have a small snack, play outside for half an hour, come in and eat our early supper, and then complete our homework in its entirety before we were allowed to watch our favorite television shows. I forgot to write the poem in our homework time, so as we watched *Lost in Space,* I sneaked to scrawl something quickly in front of the television.

I only remember the first line of the poem that I composed. As I am a bit of a hoarder, it is likely that, in a few years or so, I will find the now 54-year-old poetry submission. But the first couplet went like this:

Three Wise Men came bearing gifts, we're told.
The gifts were frankincense, myrrh, and gold.

Sister collected all of our assignments the following morning. Without asking for our permission, or notifying us, Sister submitted our work to the Archdiocesan Poetry Contest. To my shock as much as Sister's, I won second place. Again, my parents and I were invited to an event to celebrate the winning submissions. However, this time I was ready. It was *my* work, even if the nearly forgotten assignment was hastily written while I was watching *Lost in Space.* When my name was called, I got up, read my poem, and once again was handed an envelope. This time as Sister jumped up to relieve me of my two-dollar prize, I quickly handed it to my mother and asked her to put it in her pocketbook. Sister was red with rage. I smiled sweetly at her.

The best revenge I ever got on Sister Miseria was entirely unintentional on my part. As much as I didn't like Sister, when she and the other nuns asked for volunteers to wash the classroom boards, distribute morning milk and collect the milk money, or help clean the convent, I always volunteered.

The nuns' private spaces were likely smaller than prison cells. They had just enough space for a single bed, a small bureau, and a bookcase, with harsh overhead lighting. There was barely room even for the minimal belongings each nun owned. Everyone in the convent shared a small storage space, so extraneous items were limited. One afternoon, four other volunteers and I went to the convent with Sister Miseria to wash floors, clean the bathrooms, dust, and vacuum. We worked for two hours or so. When Sister was about to dismiss us she gathered us together. She was holding a beautiful 16-inch statue of the Infant of Prague. In addition to the beautiful brocade cloak on the statue, the statue came with six additional cloaks in a range of rich colors. The statue had different finery for each day of the week. It was breathtaking!

Sister had received the item as a gift and had no space to store it, so she had to give it away. Since we were faithful in our assistance in the convent, and although she still disliked me intensely, she decided to be fair about how to determine who got the statue and its accoutrements. Sister instructed us to each choose a letter of the alphabet and tell her our choice. She waited until all of us had responded before she announced the winner. I did notice that her face contorted with anger as I answered, but she didn't say anything. After we finished, she thrust the statue and the brocade cloaks into my arm, saying with fury, *"You won!"* The letter was "J" for Jesus. Oops. I had narcissistically chosen "J" for Judy and the statue was mine!

My mother was rather doubtful when I got home that Sister Miseria had given me such an elaborate gift, until I explained how I won. My saintly mother suddenly snickered (she said it was a cough) and asked if she could keep the Infant of Prague on display on the mantel in our parlor. I was proud to accede to my mother's wishes. After all, her name (Jean) also began with a "J"!

In late winter, my parents informed Kathy and me over supper that we were going to take the entrance exam for Girls' Latin School. It wasn't a question. We were told, and we were expected to pass, as it would be a privilege to attend one of the highest-rated exam schools for young women in the country. My initial thought was that if I didn't take the entrance exam, I would not have to transfer schools again. Then the reality struck that I would be away from Sister Miseria if I got into Latin. Kathy and I were both accepted, and never could have anticipated the "adventures" that the next two years would bring.

13

⚬⚬

Girls' Latin School and Society

G irls' Latin School was established in 1877 on West New-
ton Street in Boston with the intention of giving classical
education and college preparatory training to females. It
was the first girls' preparatory high school in the United States.
As well, in 1888, the Girls' Latin School newspaper was created,
and titled *Jabberwock*. The newspaper secured the permission of
Lewis Carroll to use the name of his poem, "Jabberwocky," famous because of its importance in the 1871 novel *Through the
Looking Glass*, Carroll's sequel to *Alice in Wonderland*. *Jabberwock* is one of the oldest school newspapers in the United States.

A primary goal of GLS was to prepare the students for college admission to Ivy League colleges and universities. Instead,
my undergraduate admission was to Boston State College, which
has its own connection to Girls' Latin.

In 1907, Girls' Latin School shared a brand-new building
with Boston Normal School on Huntington Avenue. Although the
original building is now part of Massachusetts College of Art, the
name "Girls' Latin" is still inscribed over one of the entrances to
the building. When Boston Normal School expanded to become
Boston State College, Girls' Latin was forced to move to the old
Dorchester High School for Girls in Codman Square. I attended
Girls' Latin in the Codman Square building, and oddly enough,

later graduated from Boston State College in the location where Girls' Latin had once shared space with it.

My mother had attended Dorchester High for Girls in the same yellow brick building in Codman Square. My mother, and my sister Kathy, and I all had the same headmistress: Miss Margaret Carroll, who served Girls' Latin from 1966 to 1978, and before that, Dorchester High for Girls, where my mother graduated in 1951.

I entered Girls' Latin School in the seventh grade, and my sister Kathy entered in the ninth grade. Girls' Latin had a reputation for academic excellence. We were repeatedly reminded, on admission, that it was a great honor to have been accepted. In fact, we were offered, often and insistently by our teachers, school bags emblazoned with the Girls' Latin name and logo, while being informed that their cost was secondary to the status that carrying the bag would confer. My mother, as a modest woman, would not allow us excessive pride in ourselves, so we carried our usual plain canvas school bags, although the number of books we had to carry back and forth to school each day for our five- to six-hour average nightly homework assignments wore through the fabric quickly. Kathy and I developed strong arms and backs but weakened spirits from the discouragement of our inaugural year at Latin.

I recall sitting in a classroom in the seventh grade. Despite the rigor of the school, I had begun to love it. That does not mean that there were not select teachers that I despised. These "unfair" teachers were the ones that I resented for not automatically giving me As on my report card, as I had always gotten in parochial school. (I did spend an inordinate amount of time in the school library. Unfortunately, I was socializing more than studying.)

I bonded quickly with so many of the other students because we had a common opponent, the curriculum. I was for the first time exposed to an extraordinarily diverse population, relative to ethnicity, social class, and religion. The criteria for admission to Girls' Latin School were residence in Boston, passing the admissions test, and having a stellar academic record. Every moment of our days was caught up in just trying to survive academically.

Although racial conflict was a significant issue in the United States at large, and at home in Boston, at Girls' Latin School, it never seemed to be a part of the culture. Instead, all students shared a common challenge: surviving academically and being promoted to the next year. Although my sister and I had come from primarily white, Irish Catholic parochial schools and had had very little interaction with people of other races or cultures, we melded almost seamlessly with many Chinese students, Jewish students, black students, and others, and the diversity of the population strengthened our social relations.

However, that changed for me dramatically and unexpectedly one Monday. I was standing at my locker when a black girl that I barely knew approached me and told me in no uncertain terms that she was going to kill me after school. She didn't give me a reason why she threatened me. In fact, it seemed to be much less a threat, and instead, a promise. I was scared to death. I did not know the girl personally. I had never spoken either to or about her prior to this declaration, and I had no idea how to respond. I was distracted all day about what would be my fate when school let out. In the many intervening years between this episode and now, I have questioned so much about the event. Perhaps she, as a black girl experiencing daily racial disparities, wanted a white girl to feel the fear that she lived with every day. I'll never know.

My instinct was to flee, not to fight. However, I couldn't call home to ask my mother to dismiss me and pick me up. My mother had no car, and she was home caring for then four-year-old Christine and one-year-old Scott. It was unlikely that Miss Carroll, the headmistress, would even have allowed me to call my mother. As well, the code of the streets and elsewhere was not to tell on people. One was seen as a rat for tattling, especially when I had not been physically harmed.

I did, in all honesty, fear for my life, enough so that it crossed my mind to disregard the rule to call my father from work to come pick me up, in order to save my life, as I interpreted the threat as a sincere statement of intent.

And here is what I find ironic: I was truly more reluctant to interrupt my father during his workday than to face what I believed to be certain death after school. I made the conscious decision to let fate decide the outcome.

I would never even have considered talking to a teacher or guidance counselor about this threat. I finally decided that I was helpless to do anything at all, and I proceeded through the day in abject fear.

Inexplicably, when I arrived back at my locker at the end of the day, the young woman who had threatened to kill me approached me. She gave me a half smile, and said, "You're all right. I'm not going to kill you." I have never known what changed her mind. Perhaps she found out from others that I had never expressed any animosity or derision about her, and that I didn't deserve the fate she had promised me. I never had an experience like that again. I was relieved. If there was a lesson to take from that, it was that some misunderstanding had likely occurred. Contrary to my typical response to challenges, I did not fight back. I did not escalate the situation, and things calmed down. I was so relieved when she told me that she was not going to fight me, that I just thanked her and walked away. That was enough for me.

Another way racial tensions showed up for me during my time at GLS concerned a huge misapprehension I later found I was under regarding Malcolm X. His exact role in the civil rights movement was confusing to me at the time, and his early political statements and actions, as I misunderstood them in my childhood, caused me nightmares and increasing panic about how to escape the ubiquitous violence. Let me explain: My brother Scott Andrew was born in September 1967 when I was 13. Scott and I were both "lily-white, blue-eyed blond" children. At the time of Scott's birth, I had just started eighth grade at Girls' Latin and I spent a great deal of time in the school library. I had earned the stigma of a "flunkie" from two failing grades my first year at GLS. The best way I could think of to repair my tattered image with my fellow students was to lug around with me during the entire school day the biggest, heaviest book I could find—the *Official Report on the Assassination of President John F. Kennedy,* weighing in at nearly 3 pounds. It felt like 20.

I borrowed it from the library and renewed it for months, till my arms could no longer bear the strain, and I had convinced myself that now everyone was certain that I was actually very smart. In the library, however, I also began to read local and national newspapers. Still buttressing to my intellectual reputation, these were easier on my arms and back, and prepared me well for the supper-table social and political discussions required by my father.

But the news was dismal, and racial and ethnic tensions were high in our country. Reading the newspapers educated me but also gave me nightmares.

I was especially fearful of the American Muslim minister Malcolm X I read about who was a human rights and civil rights activist best known for his early controversial advocacy of black supremacy. I knew little about him except that he had been a devout follower of the Nation of Islam and its leader Elijah Muhammad, who vocally opposed integration and the pacifist philosophies of Martin Luther King, Jr.

One of the most important things I didn't know in 1967 about Malcolm X was that he had been assassinated on February 21, 1965. But especially, I was terrified for my life and baby Scott's based on a phrase that replayed in my head each time I looked at my precious infant brother: "Malcolm X is going to kill all the lily-white, blue-eyed blonds." That was us. I was convinced that Malcolm X would find and murder us both.

I knew my parents would oppose the plan that I had developed while I quivered in fear each night. I would pack up enough clothing for the baby and me and sneak off, running away to save our lives. I had to remember diapers and bottles, as well.

My plan was not hypothetical. I had actually written a list of the supplies I needed to sustain us when I executed my plan to run away in the night with baby Scott. I sincerely thought that was the only hope for the two of us in the family with fair skin, hair, and blue eyes to escape being murdered at the hands of Malcolm X. Though always an anxious person, I never asked anyone for help of any sort. In my mind, I believed that I could figure things out for myself, and so the plan was to escape to save us both. But I also was aware of the likely futility of taking an infant and being on the run, without money, clothing, housing, or other necessities of life. Thus, I reluctantly abandoned my plan. I decided that Scott and I just had to stay at home and fervently pray not to be murdered.

I later learned that the "Lily Whites," instead of being people like Scott and me, were a sub-section of the Republican party organized against African-Americans' socioeconomic and political gains achieved during Reconstruction. What turned out to be the truth of the matter was that, under the influence of the Nation of Islam, Malcolm X *had* indicted white America in harsh terms for its crimes against black Americans. At that time, he *did* advocate black supremacy, and the separation of black and white Americans. However, in the 1960s, he began to grow unhappy with the Nation of Islam, and in particular with Elijah Muhammad. Ultimately, Malcolm X separated from the Nation of Islam and embraced Sunni Islam. When he went to Mecca, as Maya Angelou recounts, he said, "I have met white-skinned, blue-eyed men who I've openly called brother. I was wrong." Angelou summed up, "Now it takes a great deal of courage to say that."

GLS had an extremely strict code of dress and conduct. It applied if you were on school property at any time. Even in the dead of winter with snow three feet deep on the ground and falling, we were not allowed to wear long pants under our dresses and skirts. Since an otherwise unusual exception item to the dress code was allowed, a brief explanation is in order: We *were* allowed to wear plastic bread bags over our shoes—but only *under* our boots. The reason for the plastic bags was efficiency. Wearing bread bags over your shoes, especially when arriving at school on snowy mornings and having to be in the classroom before the bell rang, speed was of the essence. Bread bags were quicker to take off than overshoes. Little time was wasted before yanking off the outer footwear and tossing them into the locker.

The dress code was for girls to be in clothes suitable for school, most typically skirts, blouses, cardigans, and knee-high socks. The only exception was when we donned our royal blue gym bloomers (with names hand-embroidered on the right hip, whether or not we knew how to embroider). With the bloomers, we wore short-sleeved white middy shirts, white ankle socks, and sneakers. The moment the whistle was blown, signaling the end of gym class, we all beat a hasty retreat to the locker room to get out of the embarrassing uniforms. There was no exception to school rules. Even if gym class was held during the last period of the day, one had to return to street clothes for dismissal.

Another inviolable school rule was that stairs were labeled "up" or "down" staircases to facilitate traffic patterns. This was complicated by the fact that there was a huge hole in the middle of the fourth floor that was never repaired while I went to school in that building. So if you were in a classroom on one end of the fourth floor, you had to go down a "down" staircase, walk the length of the intact third floor and then up an "up" staircase to get to your next fourth floor classroom. The fact that there was no running allowed in school made the task of just getting to the next class on time even more onerous.

Science and Latin however, not gym or stairway selection, were to be my (temporary) undoing. I loved my science teacher and was far more interested in his ability to entertain us than to motivate us to learn. I was particularly fascinated when he brought a rifle to school to demonstrate principles of physics, and he shot a sharpened pencil through a two-by-four piece of wood. I loved rifles, as my father had taught me how to shoot in the cellar of our Edwin Street home. My father had a workshop in the cellar, but also used the space for target practice. Together we blacked out the tiny windows with paint to obscure anyone's view inside. My father would load the rifle and stand behind me supporting my shoulder against the kickback and tell me when to shoot. I thoroughly enjoyed it. However, I was just a stand-in until my mother reluctantly allowed my brother little Lonnie to pick up a BB gun. My days of shooting were over. My father had his son with whom to shoot. But I remained fascinated with my science teacher's experiment, and did, in fact, heed his caution to "not try this at home." (And he didn't even know that I had access to both rifles and sharp pencils!)

The short story is that, despite my fascination with rifle physics, I failed science. The final straw may have been when I learned, to my horror, during lunch that I had forgotten that we had a science project due that very afternoon, immediately after lunch. I was never able to stick my fingers down my throat to induce vomiting, so there was no way I was going to be able to be sent to the nurse's office instead of class. I made a sudden, capricious decision to do a science project during lunch and submit it 30 minutes later. I had an apple. That was a start. I didn't have a knife, but I had a key to my locker. I used the locker key to cut the apple in half. There were seeds. That was scientific. I handed in the two uneven halves of the apple, now turned brown, to the science teacher on entering the classroom. This gave a whole new, negative meaning to giving an apple to the teacher. He was usually a friendly fellow, but his smile turned upside down when I told him that this was my (spontaneous) science project. He handed back my garbage, informed me that it was unacceptable, and did not even crack a smile to indicate that he was joking. Drat! Foiled again.

So that explains, in part, how I got an E in Science in 7th grade. I tried futilely to convince my parents that it stood for "Excellent", but my numerical grade indicated otherwise. The standard F for a failing grade, and even a Red F (the worst!) was likely preferable to a Latin School E.

My failure in Latin class was another head-hanging occasion. Latin was considered a "dead language" that apparently was alive and thriving where I went to school. and yet I couldn't master it. Rather, I didn't put in the effort or the conduct required for a passing grade.

Initially, I simply didn't get it. First of all, classical Latin was very different from the ecclesiastical Latin I had grown up with. I could recite all of my prayers in Latin. I knew God's phone number. It was *et cum spiritu tuo* (that is, "et cum spirit 2-2-0," "and with your spirit"). Please pardon the Catholic children's joke. *Mea culpa, mea culpa, mea maxima culpa*. And yet I failed Latin!

The most immediately noticeable difference between the two types of Latin is the pronunciation. Typically, "church Latin" (ecclesiastical Latin) is pronounced with Italian pronunciation rules. Therefore, words like *caelum* (sky) are pronounced "chay-lum," whereas classical Latin calls for it to be pronounced, "ky-lum." Words like *coepit* (he/she/it begins) are also pronounced with a "ch" sound in ecclesiastical tradition ("che-pit"), whereas the classical tradition pronounces it with a hard "c" sound ("co-eh-pit" in three syllables). The oft-quoted phrase, *veni, vidi, vici* (I came, I saw, I conquered) uses the Italian hard *v* sound and the soft *c* sound ("vaynee, veedee, veechee"), whereas classical Latin calls for a *w* sound for *v*, thus making the phrase at GLS "waynee, widdy, wicky." The old graduates of Girls' Latin mostly only remember *Arma virumque cano* ("I sing of arms and the man," the opening line of Virgil's *Aeneid*).

My basic abilities were not flawed. The greater problem was that I allowed my mind to wander the entire class period every day. Sometimes I spent the class period coloring my grocery-store paper-bag book covers; other times I held my faceted ring right up to my eye and marveled at the ways that the refraction allowed me to see outside the window. The teacher could not possibly have missed that I wasn't paying attention.

I, along with my friends Mary and Pat, had also managed to get into trouble with our teacher Mr. Latham before classes had even begun. Mary Kiernan, Patricia Kennealy, and I had become fast friends shortly after we met at GLS. Because we lived in different parts of the city, we rarely had time to just spend together enjoying our growing partnership. We hit on the idea of coming to school each morning as soon as the janitor unlocked the doors. Then we could laugh and talk and play, as kids in neighborhood schools got to do all the time.

One early morning when Mary, Pat, and I arrived early just to have some friendship time, we were fooling around thinking that no one else was in the building besides us and the janitor. Mary, Pat, and I were running up a flight of stairs when one of my shoes slipped off. Jokingly, my friends kicked the shoe back down the stairs and I chased it to retrieve it. As Mary and Pat laughed from the landing, I leaned over to pick up the orphaned shoe, and heard a voice booming angrily over my head. *"Girls! Girls!"* Mr. Latham screamed at us. *"This* is a school building, *not* a gymnasium! And furthermore, Miss Kirwan, you were running *down* an *up* staircase!"

We were scared to death, assuming that he was either going to kill us in his state of fury, or report us to Miss Carroll, the stern headmistress. *"In my classroom now!"* he commanded, purple in the face." We all held back our tears, but slunk side-by-side along the hallway, unsure of what fate awaited us. After he yelled some more, he threatened to bring us to the headmistress immediately to be expelled. Then he stroked his chin thoughtfully, and said, "I'll give you one more chance. I will give you a list, and you will complete eight declensions and eight conjugations by the end of the day. Hand them in completed and correct, and I won't report you. If you fail at this, you will be gone!"

I know that he fully expected that at least I would fail the assignment, nevermore to be a problem for him. He would have trusted Mary and Pat to successfully complete the punishment. I worked frantically in every free moment. I barely breathed all day. I denied my bodily urges for the cafeteria, the water bubbler, and the bathroom. I wrote, and wrote, and wrote, and wrote, between classes, under my opened desktop during classes, and as I walked through the halls when changing classes. I finished on time, as did Mary and Pat, but I know that I had not had even one moment to spare. When we turned in our work at the appointed moment, Mr. Latham slowly read each person's assignment, mine last, of course. He looked with satisfaction at what Mary and Pat had done. Then he glanced at mine and became nearly apoplectic to see that I too, had completed the work correctly on my own. There was no opportunity to cheat, nor the time, nor the inclination, given the stakes attached to the assignment. All of this for childplay early in the morning when we actually didn't even realize that all usual school rules did not get suspended outside of the official hours of attendance.

However, it was embarrassing to keep getting failing grades in Mr. Latham's classroom. I had learned too late how to remediate my effort problem as well as its solution: to study, and to ask for extra help. I picked up the Latin primer at home and read, and read, and practiced, but I would not and could not ask Mr. Latham for help. As nearly every student having difficulty mastering a subject believes, I too believed simply that "Mr. Latham hates me. That's why he keeps flunking me."

We would have quizzes every day, and the following day he would slam down my poorly performed work onto my desk and look at me with disgust. But I had caught on to the puzzle: Latin had an order to it. I studied the patterns and rules, the vocabulary, learned my conjugations (a system for organizing verbs) and declensions (a system for organizing nouns) and the vocabulary. And then I took my next quiz. Before he even pulled the completed test out of my hand, he rolled his eyes and asked me sardonically, "Miss Kirwan, do you ever study?" I didn't answer. The next day he put the corrected quiz on my desk face down. I confidently looked at it. I had earned an A. However, I had figured out how to achieve success in Latin too late to save that school year. As previously stated, I failed for the year, went to summer school, and mastered as much of the language as they could throw at me. Even after I left Girls' Latin School, I continued to study Latin, the language that was anything but dead to me. By tenth grade, I translated the original *Aeneid* from Latin to English. And when I took my Latin Achievement tests for college admission, I scored a 700 out of 800, a very high score. I received a commendation as a Latin scholar.

Kathy had had her own academic challenges in ninth grade at GLS. In the spring of our first year at Latin, our parents received letters that we both had earned Es in two classes. Despite Kathy's effort in addition to mine to convince our parents that "E" was for the highest grade allowed to be assigned, they understood that the grading scheme at GLS required that E, rather than F, be granted for failing grades. In order to continue at GLS, we would have to go to summer school. I thought that the humiliation would actually kill me. It didn't. Together Kathy and I took the train and trolley from home to Avenue Louis Pasteur, where Boston Latin (the boys' school) was situated. It turned out that it made more sense financially to combine the summer school classes at Boys' Latin. Like Jennifer Warnes and Bill Medley sang in the movie *Dirty Dancing*, in the summer of 1967 *I had the time of my life*: Nestles Crunch bars from Sparr's Drug Store on the corner of Huntington and Longwood Avenues; wearing shorts to school; and smart, good-looking boys were all critical elements. Interestingly, the boys did not prove to be a distraction. Since we were all in survival mode, we did not give in to behavior typical for girls at that time to hide their intelligence from boys. Society told us that boys liked dumb, pretty girls. We were too smart to buy into that stereotype, and we competed with the boys for classroom success. We all won.

When I began summer school, I discovered that one of my fellow GLS flunkies was a young woman with whom I had attended kindergarten at Rochambeau School in Dorchester. We joined up with a third girl and became a terrific trio. While we played and laughed and fooled around a lot during our commute and on brief session breaks, we were determined to go back to Girls' Latin School. During summer school at Boston Latin School, we learned how to learn. Our remedial lessons reinforced how to participate in class, study, and perform successfully. As well, we achieved the ability to consistently earn As at Girls' Latin School. Kathy and I excelled in our second years. We both hoped to graduate from the illustrious institution. But life had other plans.

My sister and I sailed through our second years at GLS but were soon informed by our parents that we would be moving out of the city in the fall of 1978. I was devastated. In my state of mind at this terrible news, I could not summon up the ability to appreciate how my two years at the school had provided me with lessons and memories that I would never forget. Over the many subsequent years, however, I have fondly recollected episodes and experiences from my two years at Girls' Latin. As well, the teaching methods at Latin (both Girls' Latin and summer school at Boston Latin) have had a profound influence on how important rigorous effort is in becoming successful in any field or endeavor in life.

Still, the news that the family would be abruptly leaving Dorchester and moving to the suburbs shook me to the core. Perhaps recognizing how difficult I was finding this change, my parents uncharacteristically allowed me more freedom initially in South Weymouth. They understood and supported my need to keep returning to Dorchester to be with my friends. I sometimes showed up at Girls' Latin at the end of the school day to reconnect with favorite teachers. I recall hanging around on the side stairway on Talbot Avenue, the main exit from the school, and being fondly greeted and hugged by those who were privileged to still be at Girls' Latin.

But my parents had a limit to their patience. My sister Kathy had gotten a job at Bea's Bakery in Columbian Square in South Weymouth shortly after we had moved into the new house. When she left the job for a better paying opportunity at the local supermarket, my parents told the owner, without consulting me, that I would replace my sister in her job at the bakery. So much for free time to prolong my adjustment to leaving Dorchester. I was now employed after school and on weekends. I kept in touch with my Latin School friends by phone and with occasional sleepovers, but as time went by, I adapted to my new life.

Now that I had employment that I had not anticipated, I did what any smart kid does. I got a job at the bakery with me for my best friend, Barbie Donnellan. We nearly brought Bea's Bakery to collapse with our hijinks. Yes, when the boss was away, we certainly did play. And the primary recipient of my trickery was no one other than Mr. Latham, my archenemy from Girls' Latin School. Neither of us had any idea the other resided in South Weymouth. He could not possibly have anticipated that the girl he had treated so disparagingly would ever be handling his food.

When Mr. Latham walked into Bea's bakery and we spotted each other for the first time, we both gasped. And then my eyes narrowed. I was the only clerk on duty, and so he had to speak to me if he wanted baked goods. It would have been safer for him to have gone down the street to Purity Supreme supermarket. So, we both gritted our teeth and said hello. We exchanged small talk, rather forcedly, and he placed his order. I tied up the box neatly after packing up his pastries. They came with a bonus—a few finger holes poked in his pies. They were hardly discernible, but I knew they were there. He came back to Bea's Bakery again and again. *Erat autem vir fortis* (he was a brave man). I never actually did anything to his food that would qualify as adulterating it. I would never adulterate anything with him! I did stay within public health guidelines in the handling of his desserts. His just desserts. I assume, however, that he never really enjoyed Bea's Bakery after he discovered that I worked there. *Veni, vidi, vici.* I came, I saw, I conquered!

14

⁓

Catholic Church Leadership During My Teen Years

The Pope of the Roman Catholic Church when I was a child was John XXIII. John XXIII had very advanced ideas of what the Catholic Church should be and do. His views on equality were summed up in the following statement: "We are all made in God's image, and thus, we are all Godly alike."

The Second Vatican Council, more commonly known as Vatican II, was intended to bring the archaic practices and principles of the Roman Catholic Church into conformity with those of the modern world. As Pope, John XXIII's primary objective was to improve relationships between Catholics and their religion, one that was becoming less relevant in an age of dramatic social change. One of the historic changes wrought by Vatican II was that Mass began to be celebrated in people's own languages rather than Latin. Pope John Paul did not live to see these changes to completion. He died in 1963 and was canonized (canonization is the process in the Catholic Church by which the Pope venerates a deceased person to the status of saint) alongside Pope John Paul II on April 27, 2014.

Deeply devoted to the Catholic Church, our family was very gratified by many of the progressive changes brought about by Vatican II. We had long held beliefs contrary to those espoused by the church prior to Vatican II that people of other religions were inferior to Catholics. After Vatican II, we accepted the celebration of the Mass in English, although for our entire lives, we had known only Latin Masses. Celebration of the Mass in the language of the people served allows those participating a much more thorough understanding of, and involvement in, each part of the Mass. However, many of us miss the tradition of the Latin Mass; fortunately, designated churches still offer Latin Masses for those of us who wish to partake in the original and familiar tradition.

As a Catholic family, we welcomed the modernization of attitudes toward women in the religious orders. After Vatican II the religious sisters were no longer mandated to wear the full "habit," or voluminous garb, as they had for centuries. Younger nuns, in particular, adopted simple monotone skirts, matching jackets, and unadorned blouses. A veil, even a short one, was no longer required, but in the transition period, most of our younger nuns still opted for a head covering with the modest clothing to set them apart as nuns. Likewise, they achieved a much greater degree of freedom in the community. While nuns were no longer limited to traveling either in pairs or with a lay chaperone, in the transition many did so. Even with Vatican II, however, nuns played a minimal role in assisting at Catholic Masses. It would be many years until female lectors and altar servers would be welcomed onto the altar.

For many decades, Catholics had been required to abstain from eating any food or consuming any beverage except sips of water prior to being served Holy Communion at Mass. This was to prepare the body spiritually and physically to receive Holy Communion. The initial requirement had been that fasting should commence on the prior midnight before Communion was to be received. In the early 1960s, the rule was limited to fasting for three hours before receiving "the host" (the Communion wafer) to lessen the chance of Catholics fainting in Mass due to the physical stress of the earlier restrictions. In the later 1960s, the rule was relaxed further to require only a one-hour fast before being administered Communion. An exception was nearly always granted for those who needed to take food or water with medication prior to going to Mass.

Another part of the tradition was that lay members of the community, including the Communion recipient, could never touch the Host (the consecrated wafer). This caused a literal sticky situation as the dry bread wafer often stuck to the roof of the mouth once the priest deposited it on the person's tongue. It was not uncommon to see many people, particularly children, making odd faces as they wrestled the now sticky-with-saliva wafer from the roof of the mouth. Hands seen floating up toward the mouth to pry the wafer free were quickly slapped away by nuns and/or parents, vigilant for such behavior. *"No touching the host for any reason,"* was the admonition hissed at the miscreant in the solemnity of the church.

Pertinent to this rule was an episode that brought a flurry of nuns to the altar rail nearly prostrate from profound distress. A young girl had opened her mouth to accept Communion from the priest, but she failed to close her mouth and swallow the wafer. Instead, as she headed back to her seat, the girl coughed and accidentally expelled the wafer which hit the floor. The consecrated Communion wafer was to be untouched by any hands other than that of the priest. As many others were leaving the altar rail at the same time, and may have unwittingly stepped on the sacred wafer, nuns descended in droves, waving white hankies and dropping to their knees in a rush to cover the precious Body of Christ (the Holy Communion wafer). The priest stopped the Mass to perform the appropriate ritual to recover and correctly dispose of the wafer. Muffled murmurs of Mass attendees reverberated throughout the church because of this unusual event. The girl was marked for life by the other young witnesses who never failed to point out the one who had "coughed out God onto the floor of the church."

With changes in Church policies and practices, it later became acceptable for Catholics to receive the consecrated host (the "body of Christ") in their hands, place the wafer on their own tongue, and then also to sip the wine (the "blood of Christ") from the community chalice.

As Catholic children, we were allowed to partake of a sip of wine in church from about 13 years of age or so. My first taste of wine was at a Catholic retreat for young teens. During the small group Mass, we all stood in a circle around the priest for Communion. He administered the Communion and then handed each of us the chalice. I have always been germ-phobic but couldn't fathom how I might refuse to drink the Holy wine in such an intimate setting. I took a gulp. An immediate pleasurable sensation filled my body from that one swig. I thought, "There is a God!" I had to hold back from taking a large second mouthful of wine. This was my very first taste of alcohol and at the time all I could think was how nice it was to be Catholic. However, the germaphobe in me won, and I never sipped wine from a communal vessel again in my life. What a difference a clean glass would make!

As I mentioned, a change due to Vatican II that had very personal meaning to us was the acceptance of other religions as equal in importance to Catholicism. We had been taught by the nuns that only Catholics could go to heaven. We were discouraged from playing with children who attended public school, because they were assumed to be non-Catholic and therefore "pagans." Two episodes from my childhood illustrated how strong the effect of these teachings were on us. The first involved one of our very favorite uncles who, despite having seven of his own children, loved to be surrounded by kids. We spent a great deal of time with the Sullivan family, and it wasn't unusual for Uncle Paul to gather up as many cousins as his car would hold and take us for a swim at the Codman Square YMCA pool on a Sunday afternoon.

Having been one of the bunch of swimmers on a particular Sunday, we got home too late for me to set my hair in pin curls. I went to bed and was yelled at for coming in "out of uniform" on Monday morning. When Sister asked me why my hair was not curled, as required, I explained that we had gotten home late from swimming and had to go directly to bed after bathing the previous evening. Sister had a fit, screaming, *"Young Men's Christian Association? YMCA? You went swimming at a Protestant organization? You are never to do that again!"* I was humiliated and confused. None of the swimmers had seemed to be pagans. I related the story to my mother, and she (a deeply devout Catholic) was furious at Sister. My mother tersely explained to me that despite the fact that we were Catholic, we did *not* consider anyone to be inferior to us. I was educated and elated! We could still go swimming at the Y with Uncle Paul and the cousins.

The second episode involved a friend of my mother, with whom she worked part-time. Anne Wong was a young, single woman. We children were very surprised that my mother had a single friend, as all of her friends were married with children. My mother invited Anne to lunch at our home, and we kids eavesdropped on their conversations. After Anne left, we (her Catholic elementary school children) informed my mother that we did not approve of her friendship with this girl. Impertinently, we told my mother that her friend was inappropriate. She asked us in a fury, "Are you saying that because she is Chinese?" Stunned, we all said, "Chinese? No. But she said she's Protestant!" Again, my very Catholic mother was enraged. She said again that she did not send us to Catholic School so that we could feel superior to non-Catholics. Hats off to my mother! We had never realized our quiet mother had such strong and morally correct social opinions.

Unfortunately, although the changes from Vatican II were dramatic at the time, they did not proceed with the times. In the year 2020, there continues to be in the Catholic Church a disavowal of those who identify as lesbian, gay, bisexual, transgender, or queer. Heterosexuality is considered to be the only acceptable standard for Catholics. This remains a significant bone of contention among many practicing Catholics and the clergy. My husband and I, as practicing Catholics, have long been allies of those with orientations other than heterosexual. We have raised our own children, from very young ages, to share our complete acceptance of others' sexuality and forms of variance from what/who were considered to be the only acceptable qualities, beliefs, behaviors, and characteristics of members of the Catholic Church.

Like many Catholics all over the world, I have become a "Cafeteria Catholic"—embracing some aspects of my faith and rejecting others. I embrace many of the Bible's teachings. But I continue to struggle against the Church's failure to vigorously condemn the worldwide sexual abuse of children, nuns, and others by some unknown number of deviant priests. Further, the enabling of these criminals by transferring them to other parishes and assignments once their sexual victimization of others has been revealed is anathema to me. Prosecution and punishment for convicted offenders should be the response and defrocking not even a question.

I'm especially angry about the documented role of the Catholic Church hierarchy in covering up the crimes against the innocent. In January 2002 in Boston, the scandal of child molestation by priests that had been spreading across America hit hard. The precipitant was the release of documents by a judge regarding the case of Father John Geoghan, a defrocked priest who had been repeatedly transferred after the Archdiocese of Boston had been informed of accusations against Geoghan of abusing 130 boys over 30 years.

In Boston, our hierarchy was headed by Bernard Cardinal Law. The 2015 film about the *Boston Globe's* uncovering, in its "Spotlight Series," the massive scandal of child molestation and cover-up within the local Catholic Archdiocese revealed the central role played by Cardinal Law in the cover-up. The movie shook the entire Catholic Church to its core.

When Cardinal Law had become an archbishop in Boston in 1984, Catholics welcomed him with open arms. Harvard-educated, Cardinal Law had been an advocate for social justice for the poor and immigrants. He had campaigned for civil rights in the segregated South.

Law was preceded as Archbishop by Richard James Cushing from South Boston, the third of five children born to Irish immigrants Patrick and Mary Cushing. Richard Cardinal Cushing was on good terms with most of the Boston elite, and built cordial relationships with Jews, Protestants, and institutions beyond the Catholic community.

Cardinal Cushing officiated at John F. Kennedy's wedding in 1953, where he also read a special prayer sent for Kennedy from Pope Pius XII. Cushing baptized many Kennedy children, gave the invocation at Kennedy's inauguration in 1961, and celebrated President Kennedy's funeral Mass in 1963 at Saint Matthew's Cathedral in Washington, DC. I received the Sacrament of Confirmation from Cardinal Cushing at Saint Mark's on April 6, 1967, as did my sister Jeanie the next year.

Cushing was Archbishop during some of the sexual abuse incidents in the Boston archdiocese which were revealed publicly after his death under his successor, Cardinal Law. Law became the first high-level Catholic Church official to be accused of actively participating in the cover-up of child molestation by predatory priests. Law's death in 2019 left him mourned by few, since it had become public knowledge that Law had protected many abusive priests over many years.

When I first heard that Cardinal Law himself had been complicit in actively covering up the abhorrent practice of sexual abuse of children by so many priests in Massachusetts, I did not want to believe that it could possibly be true. My children were attending Saint Paul's Catholic School in Hingham, Massachusetts, and all three continued to graduate from Notre Dame Academy in the same town. Saint Paul's was one among numerous churches in Massachusetts where priests had been convicted of having sexually abused children, and much proof has been uncovered that Law not only knew about the abuse but in many cases transferred the sexual offender to another parish, where the crimes most often continued.

Abundant information came into both the Boston Archdiocese and the Vatican regarding allegations of abuse by numerous priests. Responses by Law and the church hierarchy were tepid, and in some cases included outright denial of the accusations. Lawsuits and criminal investigations began, and within months, 25 priests were removed from the profession. Yet evidence indicates that Law was standing in the way of full disclosure. Public sentiment, including my own, turned against Cardinal Law. Voices of the Faithful, a Catholic group comprised of parishioners (no priests), came together in response to the crisis. They demanded an investigation into Cardinal Law's failure to keep these heinous crimes from continuing. Demands for Law's resignation grew; prompted by a letter demanding the same signed by almost 60 priests, Cardinal Law acceded.

But rather than prosecution for aiding and abetting criminal behavior by molesters, Law was transferred to the Vatican. His stature was heightened in the Catholic Church, and its response was interpreted as an assault on the victims and their supporters. He left our Archdiocese facing 500 lawsuits and $100 million in damage claims, which made bankruptcy likely.

In Rome, Law was appointed high priest of one of the four most prestigious churches, the Basilica of Saint Mary Major. In exile, he was permitted to keep his powerful role in the hierarchy of the Catholic Church.

My husband and I toured Rome in 2018. In the Vatican, we visited the very large gift shop. Prominently displayed among carousels of pictures and postcards of some of the most admired Catholic figures in the world were portraits of Cardinal Law. Although I was tempted to shred them with my bare hands and throw them on the floor, the Swiss Guard were watching. Instead, I went from one display to the next, turning any image of Law so that his face did not show. The Swiss Guard watched me closely, but never intervened or even asked why I was doing this. I guessed they had seen and heard it all before.

Ultimately, we remain Catholic, while decrying the abuse and the Catholic Church's failure to monitor and intervene when abuse was reported to church supervisors. Tragically, many of the abuses were perpetuated by these hundreds, even thousands of criminal men for many years because of their transfer rather than punishment and removal. The damage to its victims, and to the Catholic Church, cannot ever be accurately assessed. Atonement by the Church and financial settlements are not enough. What the Catholic Church has brought upon itself is a significant decline in membership. Numerous parishes have closed. Others have merged two or more parishes into one. Financial remuneration to victims for injuries physical, psychic, and spiritual have depleted many millions of dollars raised for the church by the faithful.

For the Catholic Church to have any hopes of returning to be the institution that shapes the spiritual lives of its 1.2 billion members throughout the world, it seems to me that a Third Vatican Council should be called by progressive Pope Francis, if not his eventual successor. The Catholic Church will not heal until its people regain our respect and trust not only in its practitioners, but in its philosophies and practices. Lay members of the Catholic Church should have a voice on a Third Vatican Council that allows it to take into account changes that the faithful wish to see incorporated. Finally, issues most pressing to Catholics in America and abroad must be considered: reform of the church's stance on homosexuality; enhanced roles for women; revision of the mandate that priests remain unmarried; careful consideration of, and change in, doctrines on birth control; and deeper involvement in addressing social injustices throughout the world.

15

❧

French Toast, Egg Salad, and Crybaby Jeanie

My younger sister Jeanie was always quick to cry, no doubt about it. Although just eighteen months younger, she was my polar opposite in so many ways. I was blonde, blue-eyed, hale and hearty, with ready fists and a smart mouth. Jeanie of the brown hair and hazel eyes was petite, shy, and weepy.

I lived to eat. She ate to live. I learned to cook by age nine. She learned how to sit primly at the kitchen table looking waiflike and sad as I expertly flipped French toast over in the cast-iron frying pan. I had mastered the hot, pre-buttered pan, and dropping milk-and-egg-dipped Wonder Bread slices onto its sizzling surface. I waited impatiently as the French toast fried, prodding it along by repeatedly compressing the cooking slices of bread. I figured that if I flattened the French toast, that would increase its surface area, and it would cook even more rapidly. But it just started to burn. If instead, I'd flip the wet bread too soon, I'd find the eggy surface soggy and pale, and again bear down with the spatula, coaxing the bread to brown. In the meantime, Jeanie sat moon-eyed, never asking for a thing, managing to evoke pity with her frail frame.

My father would look from me to Jeanie, and then back at me, seeing a healthy horse of a girl drooling to ingest the first bites of the steaming French toast once I'd slathered it in Vermont Maid maple syrup and more butter. "Give your food to Jeanie," he would bark at me. "She needs it more than you. Give it to her now!" In disbelief, I'd turn and glare at him. I had to do it covertly or he'd smack the fresh look right offa me. I'd imagine snatching up my crisp yet gooey prize and running out the back door, gobbling my food as I tried to escape his angry reach. I knew it wouldn't work. Resentfully, I would plate my French toast for Jeanie and put it in front of her. She'd smile oh-so-innocently at me with a distinct, "Ha, ha, I won again" smirk when Dad wasn't watching. He'd then demand I make myself "some more" while she ate. "Some *more???*" I'd scream—in my head. "I didn't have *any!*" When I protested that I wasn't going to make more for myself because "I'm not hungry now!" he'd admonish me to wash all the dishes and pans (including Jeanie's) before I even thought of escaping to the backyard to play "kick-the-can-and-pretend-it's-Jeanie's-tiny-tush." I learned not to make French toast on the weekend, because it would be snatched from my hungry jaws by the unfair father who equated small stature with royal blood. I stayed mad about French toast for a long time. And yet a few years later one wayward egg salad sandwich made my heart break for my sister.

At lunchtime at Saint Ambrose, we left school, but we didn't go home. We were dismissed by grade, with the younger ones let out before the older ones. In formation, we marched down Dickens Street from the front doors of the school in sync with the cadence of military music. One day, Jeanie was heading down Dickens, brown-bagging an egg salad sandwich to be consumed at Woolworths lunch counter once we escaped Sister's watch at the corner of busy Adams Street. We would round the corner by Rexall's Drug Store and race to Woolworths to grab one of the coveted fake-leather-covered stools. On very rare occasions, we had money and thus the privilege of buying lunch. But we were guaranteed a counter seat as long as we bought a counter drink to go with our brown bag lunch.

"Choice" was a word foreign to most kids from Dorchester. Our parents supplied us with the essential nutrients to keep our bodies hardy enough for assigned housekeeping tasks, so we ate whatever was in the brown bag. Dorchester kids did not get asked by June Cleaver, "What would you boys like me to make you for to-day's lunch, or would you rather buy something good and hot from Woolworths?" We all had the same menu at home. It was "take it or leave it." If you refused the housewife's choice of provisions, what you got instead was an empty belly. Most of us woodenly consumed the peanut butter and jelly sandwich, or the tuna salad, or whatever else we were given. But our parent's assumption that we were washing our sandwiches down with a healthy glass of whole milk was often incorrect. Many of us took the opportunity at Woolworths to drink a prohibited Coca-Cola when not under our parents' watch.

That day as our fourth-grade class, helmed by my much-loved lay teacher Mrs. Dyson, followed the third-graders toward Fields Corner for release, I saw the crowd ahead of me part like the sea, loudly gagging, jumping off the curb, and hopping back on after passing some unknown and apparently nauseating substance on the sidewalk. My blood froze. I knew instantly that the distant whimpering that I heard *had* to be coming from Baby Jeanie.

I knew without being told that she had been walking with her classmates to 30 minutes of freedom in Fields Corner clutching her egg salad sandwich in a paper lunch bag which she had not carefully kept closed. She had dropped the entire sandwich on the ground. I grimaced in silent, psychic regret, imagining my sister letting her wax-paper-wrapped sandwich slip out of the lunch sack. I could *see* our mother's hard-boiled egg and mayo mixture squishing under the cavalcade of third-grade feet. I agonized anew with each little girl's "*Ewwww*, it's on my shoe!" and little boy's giggling. This was a common event: Little girls screamed each time, and young masters Finnigan and Cullivan, Flynn and O'Leary, guffawed each time, a Buster Brown stepped into the sloppy mess.

Without yet actually hearing her wail, I knew Jeanie was dying of humiliation. I knew too that she now had no lunch, and that I had to "do the right thing" and share mine with her. I writhed in empathy as I came in sight of the egg salad smeared on the bottom of a number of little girls' shoes. My classmates and I got to the scene, and I recognized the mess as indeed having been a sandwich made by my mother. To make matters even worse, the Woolworths "counter ladies" tried their level best to keep their many hungry customers happy, fed, toileted, and returned to the route back to school. An absence of both a sandwich and the "money to buy" indicated that some child was not eating.

I formulated a plan. To avoid having to listen to my wailing sister further bemoan the squashed sandwich, I would split mine with her. When I found her in the crowd, her shoulders gave her away. She was still crying. I ushered her to a newly vacated pair of seats, thrust half of my sandwich in her hand, and commanded her to "just eat!" Her response: "I don't like egg salad, and I don't want half of yours." My pity turned quickly to aggravation. In my big-sister voice, and in true *loco parentis*, I demanded she consume the proffered half a lunch, or I'd "give her something to cry about."

Crybaby Jeanie . . . cried. She cried all afternoon, wet her pants in class from distress, and at 1:30 p.m., I was summoned to walk her home for dry undies and mother comfort.

Today, I often make egg salad sandwiches. Each time, I remember this story. I still feel the twinge of sadness at the thoughts of her humiliation. And as much as my heart pinches a bit recalling the momentous-to-a-big-sister event, I still love egg salad.

The ultimate victims of the egg salad on the sidewalk episode were my own three daughters, who never took a sack lunch to school that wasn't double-bagged and stapled shut. I've been told that my own crybaby daughter used to weep in the lunchroom over her inability to open her parcel so that she could join her sisters in eating mom-made paper-bag lunches.

As well as being a tearful tot, Jeanie was very shy. In fact, she had such reticence about speaking publicly that my parents were advised to send her to the Fontbonne Academy Drama Program on weekends when she was in elementary school. This came at considerable financial burden and expense of time, as she had to be driven back and forth to Milton (10 miles each way) every Saturday for what were intended to serve as remedial classes to address her extreme reluctance to be seen or heard by anyone outside of the family.

After Jeanie completed the remedial program, she felt confident enough to ask a clerk for a product my mother had asked us to purchase after Mass one Sunday. She and I went to O'Brien's Bakery across from Saint Mark's to buy the dozen pecan buns that accompanied our weekly Sunday dinners. On entering the busy bakery, Jeanie got flustered by the crowd. "Go ahead," I prodded her, "order the pecan buns." I hadn't tricked her into this. Her completing this intimidating task was demonstration that she had succeeded in overcoming her malignant terror of talking in public.

The bakery was busy, and the young clerks were impatient. Jeanie got more nervous; I started to giggle. Jeanie could only point to the dozen uncut buns cooling on the baking rack and say to the clerk, "That." The clerk got annoyed and asked her, "You want *one*?" Jeanie, thinking that the entire pan represented one very large pecan bun, nodded. The clerk pulled off an individual piece and started to put it in the bag. Jeanie's eyes filled with tears. Mine did too, but mine were from stifling the urge to laugh. Jeanie stammered to the increasingly angry clerk, "Just *one,* but the big one!" The clerk snapped, "This *is* one!" Jeanie tried again, crying this time: "*One big pecan bun.*" The clerk pulled off another slightly larger individual pecan bun and replaced the one in the bag with it. Finally, I intervened. I said to the clerk, "She wants the entire uncut dozen!" The clerk stuffed them into a bakery box, tied it with twine, and snatched the money out of Jeanie's trembling hand, shoving the box toward Jeanie.

Although I tried (in vain) to hold back my snickering all the way home, I did at least have the generosity of spirit to keep my mouth shut when Jeanie announced proudly to my mother, "I got the pecan buns you wanted." My mother smiled at her teary-eyed daughter and said, "I'm so proud of you. The drama classes must have worked." I kept my mouth shut but I had to go into the small bedroom where the four of us girls slept and stifle my laughter in my pillow. My bun after dinner that week tasted especially sweet!

16

⚜

Bologna on Friday

On Friday, November 22, 1963, eight-year-old Jeanie and I both stayed home from school, ostensibly sick. That was extremely rare. Even more unusual was that my mother was working outside of the home for a brief period, likely earning money for Christmas gifts. In those years, children were often unattended at home, given their parents' contact information, instructions to keep all doors locked, and respond to callers that parents were "unable to come to the phone." As Fridays were meatless in the Catholic Church, Jeanie and I, freed from the bondage of our strict parents, watched television, played games, and gloried in our selection of lunch foods: We could have peanut butter and jelly, fluffernutters (marshmallow spread with peanut butter on bread), or cream cheese and olive sandwiches. I was delighted to find that we had Sunbeam bread in the house—the only kind you could neatly tear down the middle, which fascinated me—since Capitol Market had been out of our usual Wonder Bread when my mother went shopping.

Forgetting it was Friday, I made us both bologna sandwiches. Unattended, we brought our sandwiches into the den, an area where eating was prohibited. We turned on the television to top off our delightful day. We gobbled down lunch, and then looked at each other in horror while simultaneously exclaiming, "We ate meat on Friday!" Overcome with remorse, we justified absolution from the obligation because of illness. But we both knew we were honestly healthy.

As we fretted about our imagined sin, the front door unexpectedly opened, and my father walked in. We were in a state of shock. It was early afternoon and my father never got home until 4:15 p.m., precisely. Without addressing us, he slunk down in a corner chair, covered his eyes with his handkerchief, and softly sobbed.

Expressions of emotions considered to be character defects in our family included tears. My father was not devoid of them, just extremely inhibited in displaying them. I saw him cry twice in his life, and this was the first time. I didn't see him cry again until I was in my 40s when his favorite dog died unexpectedly. Seeing my father cry when I was an adult was no less upsetting to me then than it had been in childhood.

His shoulders shook. We were at a complete loss as to how to respond. How could he possibly have known that we had violated meatless Friday? And was it a sin that it would make my father weep?

He didn't attempt to offer any explanation for his shocking display of grief. I finally gingerly approached him and asked him what was wrong. He choked out, "The President is dead." Profoundly relieved that it hadn't been our bologna consumption that had caused his grief, it took minutes for his heartbreaking announcement to sink into my head and Jeanie's.

My father was finally able to tell us that President John Fitzgerald Kennedy, the 35th President of the United States, and the only Catholic leader of our country to date, had been assassinated in a motorcade in Dallas, Texas, riding with his wife, First Lady Jacqueline Bouvier Kennedy, and Texas Governor John Connolly and his wife Nellie. John F. Kennedy was fatally shot at 12:30 p.m. Central Standard Time. Our world, as we knew it, had changed in that moment.

I pinpoint that as the moment of my lost naivete. For Catholics, the age of seven is considered the age of reason. At seven, Catholic children receive the Sacraments of both Confession (as it was called at the time), and First Holy Communion. Although I had, after two years of formal instruction in the Catholic faith, received these second and third of the Blessed Sacraments (the first having been baptism), I did not feel mature in mind or spirit. With the assassination of President John F. Kennedy, our country aged immeasurably and so did I.

As children, we experienced profound grief, and a true loss of innocence. We looked to our priests, nuns, and families for support, but they were crying too. To have emerged whole through this catastrophic event would indicate one had no soul. But we still had our God and our faith, and we moved forward. My father resumed his role as the rock of the family. As kids, we had seen him falter for the first time.

John Kennedy, at age 43, was the youngest president ever elected, and the first Roman Catholic to occupy the office. Kennedy was loved by Americans and the Irish. Irish Catholic Bostonians were particularly proud because of Kennedy's connections to the city and its environs. Kennedy had been born in Brookline on May 29, 1917. His maternal grandfather, John Francis "Honey Fitz" Fitzgerald had been a state legislator, mayor of Boston, and a congressman. The collective hearts of the nation and the world were shattered. Our ability to feel happiness again seemed an impossible dream; our innocence was gone for good. And it had nothing whatsoever to do with bologna on Friday.

17

Boston: Separate and Unequal

O ur family moved to the South Shore in 1968 from Boston. "White flight" referred to the large-scale migration of people of European ancestry starting in the 1950s and 1960s from racially mixed urban regions to more racially homogeneous suburban areas. This was a time racial conflict had erupted over unequal access to resources, including a sound public education.

Boston and the country had moved through decade upon decade of racial and social inequality. During this same period, after the Second World War, the GI Bill (Servicemen's Readjustment Act of 1944) had provided a range of benefits for veterans including low-cost mortgages, low-interest loans to start new businesses, a year of unemployment benefits, and tuition and housing support for veterans who wished to attend high school, college, or vocational school. The GI bill enabled the betterment of veterans and their families.

Many veterans utilized the housing benefits. Significant numbers of veterans joined the mass suburban migration to live among other young families in single-family houses with their own backyards and cohesive neighborhood. Most of the children walked to neighborhood schools, a vast change from the mandatory busing that was on the horizon in the city of Boston. When we moved out of Boston, we moved to South Weymouth to a neighborhood in which most of the residents were, like us, originally from Dorchester.

My father's long term Savin Hill employer had moved from Dorchester to Randolph when I was a young teen. In general, it was part of the urban migration of families and businesses to the suburbs, where space was not at such a premium as it was in the city. The move paralleled white flight by individuals in many cities in the United States where racial strife was on the rise. Another factor which precipitated our move to the South Shore was that we simply had too many kids and not enough bedrooms in our generally spacious triple-deckers. When the kids became racked and stacked, with three to a bedroom, and one brother sleeping on a couch in the front hall, our housing needs demanded a home with more room.

As well, racial and other social tensions had been increasing for decades, and it became more common for one or more of us to "get jumped" going to or returning from school, to Codman Square to my grandmother's house, or to the playground. In my immediate family, being jumped had never resulted in significant bodily harm. It happened more often when one or two of us were set upon by a group of others looking to bully and intimidate, and the results were more related to fear than to bodily trauma. But after an experience of being jumped we developed nightmares, increased anxiety about being outside of our neighborhood, and increased fear of strangers.

Generally speaking, "being jumped" could be inter-racial, or intra-racial. It could be physical, sexual, and/or emotional assault. Boys jumped either boys or girls. Belligerent girls typically targeted weaker girls. The attacks could be verbal, physical, or both. Even at that, the physical nature of the attack on my own family members was usually limited to pushing and shoving, and maybe knocking down anyone appearing vulnerable. It was not even important whether there had been any prior relationship between aggressors and victims of "jumping."

Neighborhood gangs also became increasingly explosive during this period, and that brought more serious violence. A child was murdered on Templeton Street, the next street over from Edwin. The death was said to be caused by "foul play." In the neighborhoods, young boys confused by the terminology, cheered that a "foul ball" had made the news. Their misunderstanding was naïve, but the reality was tragic.

Despite the increasingly volatile atmosphere of city life, I was devastated by our separation from Boston. I loved Dorchester. I loved my home, my friends, my neighborhood, and my church. Above all, after surviving a very difficult start at Girls' Latin School, I had happily anticipated entering ninth grade at GLS. But it was not to be. Even after we moved out, I stayed glued to information about Boston, with every intention of going back to the city when my life was under my own control.

While this book is a social history of a Dorchester Irish family through "the sixties," the common understanding of that decade does not extend from January 1, 1960 to December 31, 1969. To those who lived through the era, it began with the assassination of John F. Kennedy in 1963 and ended in 1974 with the Watergate scandal, resulting in the resignation of President Nixon to avoid impeachment. This time period also produced extraordinarily significant changes in the City of Boston and beyond.

Between 1965 and 1973, research had determined that Boston Public schools were overwhelmingly segregated by race. Because the Boston Schools were maintaining this dual segregated school system, the Massachusetts State Legislature was forced to enact the Racial Imbalance Act of 1965. The RIA defined a racially imbalanced school as one with 50 percent non-white students. Unless corrective action was taken, the Boston School system could lose funding. The School Committee used stall tactics in an attempt to delay implementing the Racial Imbalance Act. The proposed solutions submitted by the School Committee did not meet the standards of the Board of Education. During the next seven years the city failed to submit a working plan.

On March 15, 1972 a federal lawsuit was filed in Boston by the Harvard Center for Law and Education against the Boston School Committee, on behalf of 15 black parents and 43 black school children. The lawsuit was *Morgan v. Hennigan*. Tallulah Morgan was a 24-year-old mother of three, and the lead plaintiff in the case. James Hennigan was the president of the Boston School Committee in 1972 when the case was filed. Morgan and the parents of the other black children accused the Boston School Committee of intentionally violating their rights under the 14th Amendment to the U.S. Constitution, because of its policy of racial segregation. The Boston School Committee's defense was always that any racial imbalance of the public schools was no fault of the committee, it was the result of housing patterns of which they had no control.

On June 21, 1974 Judge W. Arthur Garrity found that the Boston School Committee had manipulated school boundaries, thus making it appear that the school enrollment was the result of housing patterns and not *de facto* segregation. Garrity concluded, "the Boston School Committee made districting changes for the purpose of perpetuating racial segregation." Soon after, he ordered the Massachusetts State Board of Education Plan to be implemented in September of the same year.

The plan required the city of Boston to bus 17 to 18 thousand students. Along with being controversial, the plan angered the residents of South Boston. The plan called for pairing Roxbury High School, in the center of the black ghetto, with South Boston High School, located in an Irish-dominated community opposed to busing from the beginning. Residents of South Boston were told the sophomore class would mix with blacks bused in and out, and the entire junior class would be sent to Roxbury; the senior class at both schools could choose either high school.

The residents of both Roxbury and South Boston were shocked when the plan was announced. Blacks knew their children would not be welcome in South Boston. It was evident from the beginning that enforcing the plan would be difficult. Judge Garrity's decision worried the community leaders who would be responsible for implementing the plan. The Boston School Committee was not pleased with Garrity's order, and against legal advice, voted to appeal the decision.

A simple solution had been ignored. The committee could have reduced racial imbalance by redistricting or building new schools on the borders of certain neighborhoods, thereby creating mixed schools, and eliminating the busing of students.

The Boston School Committee came under court control (1974–1988) and was forced to desegregate through compulsory busing of students. South Boston, a primarily white school, did have its students bused across the city to Roxbury High School, where the reverse also happened, per the Massachusetts State Board of Education plan. The mandate for busing as well as its early implementation, particularly 1974–1976, led to a series of riots and racial protests. Ultimately, forced busing lasted for nearly 14 years.

It did, in fact, lead to demographic shifts in Boston's school-age children, but not as intended. Instead, there was an overall decline in public-school enrollment along with white flight to the suburbs. In my own case, the date on which forced busing started in Boston was my twentieth birthday, September 12, 1974. I was too old to attend Boston public schools, and yet I was there as a student at Boston State College, located at the corner of Huntington Avenue and Longwood Avenue. Although this area was not in South Boston, it was in one of many "hot spots" for disturbances to take place, as it bordered on Roxbury, the home of many of the black children bused to South Boston schools.

One Boston State academic building was located on Lansdowne Street, across from Fenway Park. The rioting in the streets due to opposition to forced busing throughout the city, precluded BSC students walking safely between campuses. For our protection, we were encouraged to ride the yellow school buses between the Huntington Avenue and Fenway campuses. Because the college transport buses were identical to the Boston School buses, the college students were indistinguishable from Boston school students. We were all potential victims of frequent bus-flipping (school buses literally turned over in the streets as part of the violent protests). If one was in the city at any given time, it was also not uncommon to come across police cruisers that had been torched in opposition to busing.

Like the violence against schoolchildren, the violence against the police made little sense. Boston Police officers and Massachusetts State Police were ever-present in the city for the protection of all during the four years in which the busing took place. One of my classmates was William Stratton, who became one of the "top cops" in America. He recalled sittjng side by-side at Boston State College during the day with classmates who got to know him well while he was in jeans and a sweatshirt. Relationships with his college chums were friendly, but to his dismay, when he was in riot gear on the second shift with the Boston Police Department, Stratton was often attacked by protesters in the streets. He said that his identity was hidden by his gear, but that he could clearly see the faces of the protestors who were attacking the police officers who were trying to maintain order. Stratton said that he often found himself scuffling with "cop-haters" in the evenings, who were his classmates during the days. He experienced serious role conflict, but even more, personal disappointment in people that he thought of as his friends and supporters. Rioting was impersonal. The cops were just another group to blame for the rampant hatred apparent during this tumultuous period in Boston.

I would like very much to have had the opportunity to present in this book the views of former Boston students who had been bused during this 1974 to 1978 social experiment. However, I never personally knew anyone who was, in fact, part of the cohort of students, either white or black, who were bused from South Boston to Roxbury or the reverse in order to achieve racial balance.

However, I taught Criminal Justice and Sociology in a small Boston-area college from 1996 to 2019, with a significant majority of my students being state and local police officers in Boston. A brief explanation is that Massachusetts had been determined in the 1960s to have the least educated police forces in the nation. In 1970, the Quinn Bill, also known as the Police Career Incentive Pay Program (PCIPP) was enacted. Participant incentives came in the form of percentage increases to their base pay depending on the degree earned: 10 percent for an associate's degree, 20 percent for a bachelor's degree, and 25–30 percent for either a master's degree or a law degree. An unanticipated consequence of this legislation was that police officers returned to school in numbers far beyond those predicted. This was costly to cities and towns participating, who bore part of the responsibility for the increases in officer salaries. However, the percentage of educated police officers serving the Commonwealth grew significantly. As a professor at a participating college, I taught hundreds of Massachusetts police between the implementation of the Quinn bill and the next two decades. One of my teaching responsibilities for many years was supervising the master's degree thesis required by the college in which I was teaching.

When mandatory school desegregation (i.e., forced busing) was begun in Boston on September 12, 1974, protests and rioting broke out throughout the city, as I've noted. Within days the rioting and violence in opposition to the Garrity plan overwhelmed the capacity of the Boston police department to control the situation. The Massachusetts state police were almost immediately deployed to Boston to assist, both in protecting the children being bused, and to maintain order in and around the South Boston and Roxbury schools. What prompted the call for state police involvement was a stabbing of a white student at South Boston High on the first day of busing. As word spread, an angry mob formed outside of Southie High and engaged in a violent confrontation with Boston Police. A Boston police cruiser was overturned and arrests were made. On that same day, a prison uprising took place at the Massachusetts Correctional Institution in Walpole. State police were called in immediately and quelled the violence. Once this was accomplished, the state police were ordered to South Boston to safeguard lives for as long as was necessary. This edict would remain in force through November of 1977 of the busing plan.

The roles of the state police in protecting Boston's bused children included motorcycle escorts for school buses going up and then down the hill to and from Southie High while angry mobs protested and hurled insults, rocks, and other objects at the buses carrying innocent kids. State police officers were assigned to the perimeter of the school, and inside the classrooms and the hallways for all the years of forced busing.

One of the master's students that I taught was a close-to-retirement state police officer, who, along with many of his current and former colleagues, had been instrumental in the overwhelming assignment for the nearly four-year period. He based his master's thesis on the entire forced busing experience. Together, my master's student and I seized the opportunity in 2009 to retrospectively survey and interview numerous state police officers who had been directly involved in maintaining safety and control in the schools, the streets, and throughout the city during that four-year period.

Overwhelmingly the responses, both qualitative and quantitative, suggested that the numerous state police officers on duty in and around Boston during mandatory school desegregation believed that the Garrity plan, overall, had been a massive failure. As a number of the less reticent police officers admitted, "It was very successful for the police officers involved who earned massive overtime over the four-year period, but little learning was accomplished by the students during this time."

In the years between 1978 and 2020, demographic changes, more than mandates to equal access to services by race, have continually altered the ethnic composition throughout the city of

Boston. For example, Saint Ambrose Church and Parish was a faith community of predominantly Irish Catholic families when I was a child in the 1950s and 1960s. By the time Saint Ambrose Parish held its Centennial celebration in 2014, more than 800 people attended. Auxiliary Bishop Robert F. Hennessy celebrated the Mass, which had parts said in English, Vietnamese, and Spanish. "Presentation of the Gifts" at this Mass and a liturgical dance represented the ethnicities of the neighborhood including Irish, Caribbean, Central American, and Vietnamese.

As well, traveling throughout Dorchester often, as I have done so often since we moved out in 1969, I have borne witness to the ethnic and sociocultural changes in neighborhoods throughout the city. Dorchester continues to be a vibrant and valuable community, although one which struggles, like so many inner-city neighborhoods, with the problems of interpersonal and institutional violence and racism. I remain optimistic that continual activism throughout our city and country, focused especially on justice for all, is the ultimate solution.

18

Dorchester Avenue

D orchester Avenue (more often called "Dot Ave") runs south from downtown Boston, via South Boston and Dorchester, to the border with Milton, where it ends. Built as the Dorchester Turnpike, it is mostly straight. Driving south past our Edwin Street neighborhood on Dorchester Avenue, we would pass the Walter Baker Chocolate Factory on the Neponset River between Dorchester and Milton. The Baker Chocolate Company was the oldest producer of chocolate in the United States. It was established when Dr. James Baker met Irishman John Hannon, a penniless, though skilled chocolatier who had learned the craft in England. Together the pair produced "Hannon's Best Chocolate" for 15 years. In 1780, Hannon's wife sold the company to Dr. Baker after Hannon left America permanently for the West Indies. Dr. Baker then changed the name to Baker Chocolate Company.

During its operation, the smell of chocolate could be detected for miles, especially if the day was overcast. Students who attended nearby Saint Gregory's School could smell the chocolate through their open windows. Nearly everyone who grew up in Dorchester has opinions and experiences to share about Baker's Chocolate Company. Most report having loved the smell, which some described as "heavenly." Former Dorchester residents recall going to Baker's Chocolate company for the free tours and attractively priced broken chocolate bars.

A former neighbor from Dorchester told me that when he was employed there, new employees were encouraged to eat all the chocolate that they wanted while they were working. He said that after two weeks of gluttony, most people were so sick of chocolate that they never wanted to eat it again.

My mother was bothered by the fact that my Uncle Bob, who worked in the candy packing room, used to boast that he'd slip chocolate bars under his coat and take them home for his kids. My mother impressed upon me that his stealing was a sin. In fact, the company had a policy that allowed workers, in addition to visitors, to take home a small number of broken chocolate bars. Pointing out that Uncle Bob's family, like ours, was large, my mother impressed upon me that what was considered "small" for other families likely varied considerably from what Uncle Bob was secreting in his overcoat for his seven offspring plus us.

As a child, I believed that instead of the Neponset River running through and around the numerous factory buildings, it was liquid chocolate. However, I was likely one of the only children who passed through Lower Mills complaining of the cloying smell. Simply approaching Milton from Dorchester, I'd feel nauseous, and would pinch my nose shut.

Dot Ave stories abound. Not all are related to alcohol, but I was always aware of the number of taverns and "package stores" in Dorchester, especially since, as a child, I never saw any actual "packages" in those windows I walked past in my childhood! I did see beer—a *lot* of beer.

As for the taverns and barrooms, we passed many while walking in Dorchester. Like most families, ours had only one car, and Dorchester was very much a walking neighborhood. And as I walked, either alone, or with my family or friends, I observed so much. In other words, I was what was often called a "nosy parker," a term for an overly inquisitive person. I was always intrigued by the discreet signs in the front windows of barrooms like Peabody Tavern that stated, "Ladies invited." I wondered, first of all, why ladies had to be invited. Could they not go in alone? Who was inviting them? If a lady was invited, was the gentleman who invited her obligated to pay for her lunch? Her tea? What if she didn't want to have tea? Could the invited lady have something else to drink like a Coca Cola or maybe even a sip of beer? When I became a lady, would I be invited to a barroom? Would I even want to go? When the doors opened as I passed, all I could smell was cigarettes and what I presume was beer.

On one occasion, when my sister Kathy noticed our landlord's car outside a bar on Adams Street as we walked home from Saint Ambrose School, she forcibly dragged me inside. She had determined to convince him that he should drive us the one additional block home from the barroom to our Parkman Street apartment. The landlord, likely humiliated by the presence of two little uniformed Saint Ambrose schoolgirls harassing him in his happy place, reluctantly agreed to do as Kathy asked. We were not rewarded at home for our industriousness seeking unnecessary assistance in a tavern from a man presumed to have consumed alcohol, and for embarrassing our landlord in the process. However, being pressed into going into a bar had been more noxious to me than the punishment we got at home.

A veritable font of stories were shared with me by my Boston police officer students I mentioned in the last chapter. Officer O'Toole, in particular, used to delight in sharing his "OFD" (originally from Dorchester) stories with me, and I reciprocated. Officer O'Toole was born and raised in Dorchester and became a police officer on his home turf. When he policed the streets of Dorchester, he was known by the moniker "Apple" to those less than fond of his aptitude for catching criminals. As a blue-eyed blond working outside, he was particularly prone to sunburns. However, it didn't take a sunny day on Malibu Beach to turn his normally pale cheeks bright red. Any strong emotions such as embarrassment, anger, or even amazement caused his cheeks to flush. Thus, he was known as "Apple." It was also convenient for those with criminal intent to refer to him as "Apple," since there were so many officers on the Boston Police Force with Irish surnames. Everyone knew who "Apple" was.

My favorite story Officer O'Toole shared was that as an adolescent, he and his friends were fascinated by how old men could sit for hours at Donovan's Bar, just drinking alcohol all day long. The young teens would run through the barroom and harass the men just to get a rise out of them. The men would totally ignore the boys, not even commenting to each other or the bartender about the hullabaloo. Officer O'Toole said that he and his buddies would persist in provoking the unfazed imbibers. When they still gave no response, the boys would run through, chanting, "*Wax museum!*" because of the lack of lifelike response from any of the figures sitting at the bar. He said the only part of the men's bodies that would ever move were the hands that lifted the drinks to their mouths. Even the bartender ignored the kids' bad behavior as youthful pranks. However, the boys were determined to get some sort of response from the group of men, and one day brought in chaise lounges and set them up in the bar to "watch the dead men." The bartender yelled, "*Scram!*" as he chased them out. O'Toole and his friends didn't see the bartender laugh as they bolted from the building. But even a couple of the plastered patrons chuckled a bit at the boys' monkeyshines, as Officer O'Toole later learned.

A favorite story my police officer students told me had to do with Dropkick Murphy. Although the name was later adopted by a very well-known Boston punk band, the original Dropkick Murphy was a Doctor of Osteopathic Medicine who never formally practiced his chosen profession. He acquired his name "Dropkick" from his legendary wrestling skills.

John "Dropkick" Murphy operated his Bellows Farms Sanatorium in Acton, Massachusetts which he had opened originally for training fighters. Soon after he opened it, however, he and his wife compassionately decided to take in alcoholics to help them safely withdraw from alcohol abuse. Bellows Farms operated as an alcohol detoxification and rehabilitation facility from 1941–1971. Once at Bellows Farms, recovering alcoholic clients were given red pajama bottoms and a red shirt that would identify them as residents of the sanatorium if they went off the property. Wearing those clothes, they would be recognized and returned to rehab in Acton. A number of senior Boston police officers regaled me with stories of red-pajamaed patrons in taverns throughout the city. Many officers commented that the Bellows Farm residents who had escaped from the Acton facility were most often found in Irish bars in Dorchester, often along Dorchester Ave. Men, even those in red pajamas, didn't have to be "invited."

Mum and Dad's Wedding, 1952

Mum and Dad

*Mum and Dad's
Wedding Day*

Judy and Baby Christine

Grandpa and Grandma Currivan

Dad and Aunt Judy

Grandpa Thomas E. Currivan

Girls' Latin School

Judy and Santa Claus

Codman Family Day

Jeanie, Lonnie,
Kathy, and Judy

Ma and Pa Kirwan

Judy's Kindergarten Picture

Kathy's First Communion

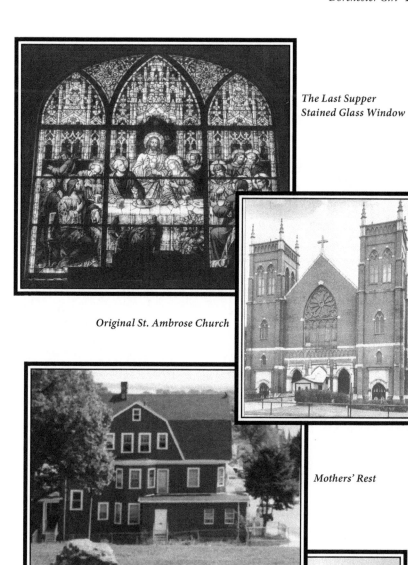

*The Last Supper
Stained Glass Window*

Original St. Ambrose Church

Mothers' Rest

Lucky Strike Bowling Alley

Kirwan Sign for Pa as
Mounted Police

Welcome to Dorchester

St. Mark's Church

Aunt Rosalie Kirwan

Thomas M. Kirwan

THE ORIGINALLY FROM DORCHESTER ASSOCIATION HAS INVITED AND ACCEPTED INTO MEMBERSHIP WITH ALL RIGHTS, PRIVILEGES, HONORS AND INSIGNIA PERTAINING THERETO:

Judith Kirwan Kelley

IN RECOGNITION OF HIGH CHARACTER AND THE GOOD FORTUNE TO BE ORIGINALLY FROM DORCHESTER, MASSACHUSETTS, U.S.A. (STILL FROM DORCHESTER ALSO COUNTS).

QUALIFICATIONS FOR MEMBERSHIP

1. BORN IN DORCHESTER, MASS. 2. LIVED IN A 3-DECKER (OR TWO-FAMILY HOUSE) 3. PLAYED HALFBALL AND TRIANGLE 4. PLAYED BASEBALL AGAINST THE STEPS OR THE CURB. 5. LIT FIRECRACKERS WITH PUNK. 6. REMEMBER ASH BARREL DAY AND THE CLOUDS AT THE ORIENTAL. 7. PLAYED INDIAN CARDS AGAINST THE STEPS AND COLLECTED FOIL FROM CIGARETTE AND GUM PACKAGES. 8. JUMPED OFF THE BRIDGE AT MALIBU, SWAM BAREASS AT TAR WHARF AND SANK ANKLE DEEP IN MUD AT TENEAN. 9. HOPPED A TROLLEY. 10. REMEMBER THE SMELLS OF WALTER BAKER AT LOWER MILLS AND THE DONUT MACHINE AT PURITAN ON OLD COLONY BLVD.

WHEREFORE THIS ASSOCIATION HAS ADJUDGED THE ABOVE MEMBER WORTHY TO RECEIVE AND DISPLAY THIS OFFICIAL CERTIFICATE, USE THE INITIALS "OFD" AFTER HIS (OR HER) NAME AND BE RECOGNIZED BY OFD-ERS WHO LIVE, WORK AND PLAY AROUND THE WORLD.

IN WITNESS THE OFD SEAL HAS BEEN AFFIXED HERETO AND ATTESTED BY ITS FOUNDER AND PRESIDENT THIS ___*4th*___ DAY OF *May* 19 *92*

S. Cosmopulos

FOUNDER AND PRESIDENT, STAVROS COSMOPULOS, OFD

94302

OFFICIAL MEMBERSHIP NUMBER

OFD © 1985 S. COSMOPULOS OFD. 8 BRIDGE STREET, NORWELL, MASSACHUSETTS 02061 U.S.A.

OFD Membership Certificate

19

❧

Fun and Games on Florida Street

When we moved from Parkman to Edwin Street, the Donnellys followed soon after, settling in an apartment on the corner of what was then Florida and Templeton Streets. (Templeton Street developed an unsavory reputation because of crime, blight, and gang activity in the 1970s, and the street was renamed Monsignor Patrick J. Lydon Memorial Street.)

Learning that our families would be neighbors again, Patrick and I resumed our friendship and tomfoolery. On the opposite corner to the Donnelly family apartment was an empty lot where Patrick and I built a fort. We played spy games all the time, sometimes inviting the younger siblings and neighbors to join in with us, and other times prohibiting them from entering our "crime domain." The biggest crime we actually committed was fabricating stories to frighten or to impress the younger kids. In fact, we both became rather talented at what might have been called "Munchausen Syndrome," a disorder named for the eighteenth-century Baron von Munchausen who entertained his dinner guests with lavish tales of his exploits, virtually all of which were the product of his fertile imagination. His stories were fantastic and impossible, as were mine and Patrick's.

We embellished our stories to the neighborhood kids even further when we sensed that we were no longer able to convince our younger listeners that we had "been kidnapped in Fields Corner but had skillfully escaped!" Our increasingly bombastic stories soon bored the younger kids. When we became too old for the fort, we abandoned it.

When I wasn't playing with Patrick and our siblings, my best friend on Edwin Street was Joanie Feeney, who lived next door to me. Joanie and I believed that we were becoming quite the mature young women, sewing side-by-side on the front porch, walking to department stores together, or seeking sage advice from her older and inherently wiser sister Breda.

Jeanie, my younger sister, was also a fun playmate, and we did more mischievous things together than those in which I could engage my older sister Kathy. One of Jeanie's and my favorite games would now be called "street harassment." Even then it might have been called "catcalling." Jeanie and I would go down Edwin to Florida Street and roam from one end to another until we spotted an appropriate prey. It was best if they were alone. We would then scoot alongside parked cars till we were a safe distance from our mark, but close enough that they could hear us when we shouted out strange things just for the purposes of flummoxing the lone walker. We would hide between cars and plan what to say, and then in turn, one of us would call out something along the lines of, "Hey Bobby! You want a date?" A somewhat interested boy, not knowing the identity of his harassers, would look around hopefully. We'd change hiding spots to confuse the kid, and go five to six feet closer, and yell the same thing. Intrigued, the poor boy would look around, and we'd yell again, "Hey Bobby! Why aren't you answering me? Do you want a date?" Poor Bobby, summoning up all his courage, would call back in random directions, "Uh, yes, I would!" We'd then respond, "Well, maybe if you hope hard enough, someone will ask you for one!" We'd then meanly collapse in giggles and run home. We were rarely, if ever, discovered.

These seem like the acts of miscreants, or at least kids who considered themselves "rats." Rats were the tough kids whose hair was slicked back with Brylcream ("a little dab'll do ya"); who wore black leather jackets, tight black pants, and pointed shoes; who smoked cigarettes and hassled passersby. "Rats" hung out in front of the Lucky Strike Bowling Alley, and on various street corners on Dorchester Ave looking and acting tough.

I was never a rat. My cohorts and I were definitely "colleege," that is, college-bound, wearing the typical brushed denim pants, madras shirts, and clean white sneakers. We wore our hair neat, glimmering from a morning shower with crystal blue Halo shampoo; we abhorred smokers and smoking; and we behaved within the limits of our parents' rules, or at the very least, as constrained by law. We hung out at Ogar's Drug Store, drinking Coca-Cola at the soda fountain while we waited for the pictures from our Brownie cameras to be developed. However, our immature street harassment was just too easy. We inflicted it, and then ran like cowards if and when we were caught. So, I guess we were *most often* colleege-like, but occasionally, we acted like little rat finks!

Another time we were playing the same semi-cruel trick, we decided to really catch the poor boy's attention by using his last name. He didn't know my younger sister, so we decided that it was she who should call out to him. She surprised me with her wittiness when she just kept yelling at intervals, "Bernardini, my name's Jeanie!" We'd watch him search, and we'd run to hide behind a different car. We'd advance six cars forward, call out the same refrain, "Bernardini, my name's Jeanie!" and then peek out to see him searching; do it once again from eight cars back, then finally tire of the game and sneak home. Jeanie and I never got caught. But Kathy and I did.

Kathy was without guile. She trusted. She wasn't a sneak, and she never expected the worst. When I told her about my games with Jeanie, she was amused. She decided to try it. We were together coming home from the dentist in Codman Square, and Kathy wanted to pull the prank. But ever a bit too innocent, she spotted two older girls a block behind us, turned around and yelled, "Hey Dreamboat!" Both smiled, and Kathy immediately yelled, "Not you, shipwreck!" I blanched. There was no trickery to this! We were in plain sight! In fact, they chased us. We were scared because they were older and bigger, and we had clearly and purposely provoked them. But with our long-ago youthful vigor (and terror of getting beaten up), we were able to outrun them and make it home safely.

My cousin Connie's responses to adolescent taunts were the best, in my opinion. When she and her sisters were subjected to insults from teenaged boys, Connie and the rest had a well-rehearsed retort: "How dare you stand there and insinuate that I should tolerate such a diabolical insult that you haven't the mental capacity to know the difference between right and wrong?" Her harassers fell silent, unable to come up with as creative a response to provocation as my female cousin had hurled at them.

My friends and I walked many miles back and forth along Florida Street in our years living on Edwin Street. We spent time with old friends, made new friends, and harassed the nasty shopkeeper, "Paul," who owned the corner market. Paul was Jewish. We had been taught in our parochial schools that we were not to associate with Protestants (who were considered to be unable to enter the kingdom of heaven and therefore "unsuitable for association with baptized Catholics") but since Jesus was a Jew, Paul was deemed worthy to provide our family's household goods. A significant problem was that Paul liked our families' business but not engaging with our families' kids who were sent to do the errands. Paul hated kids and made no secret of his animosity toward us. He called every single one of us "meshugenah" unless we had a fistful of dollars with which to purchase the items on our mothers' lists. After taking the money, he felt free to call us meshugenahs, and tell us to "go jump in a lake" unless we wanted to buy something else.

Paul was a skinflint, however. We'd catch him holding his thumb down on the scale when he weighed out the bologna; he fished out the sour pickles from the barrel with his bare hands instead of gloved hands, and he sold us overpriced comic books. Most of the kids in the neighborhood loved comic books, and one of our greatest sources of excitement was when Paul got a new supply. My favorites were the Archie Comics featuring Jughead, Betty, Veronica, and Reggie. A new comic book cost 10 cents. Paul would buy it back from us after we read it but would only give us two cents. We could then buy used comic books for five cents. I recall arguing with him about what I believed to be "highway robbery," but his spat-out response was, "I'm not a library!"

Paul's Florida Street Market's gumball machine was a form of gambling for children. Mostly, when you put your penny in the slot and turned the dial, a gumball came out the trap door. However, there were ball bearings the same size as the gumballs scattered randomly among the gum in the glass jar. If you put in your penny and got the hoped-for ball bearing, you were entitled to a five-cent candy bar. Many a kid showed troubling tendencies when they went through 25 cents in pennies trying to get one ball bearing. The 25 cents would have purchased five whole candy bars, but it was the thrill of the gamble and the ever-so-slight chance of winning that made even young kids keep playing the high-risk (for kids) game. It was like a betting parlor with only one arcade game. We'd crowd around whichever kid had pennies willing to risk, and we all celebrated when a ball bearing came out. We'd whoop and holler to Paul's chagrin, and he would try to chase us out of the store, telling us to come back alone with the ball bearing. But we persisted, all standing with the winner, suggesting the best candy bar to get for the win, and hoping that the winner would share.

The large Tootsie roll bars were good because they were scored for easy sharing, though no winner ever really wanted to share. I'd suggest helpfully that the winner get Rolos (my favorite) because they were individually packaged and could thus be easily distributed. On the other hand, I was always chagrined if the winner chose a Sugar Daddy. There was no way I was going to lick the hard caramel pop on a stick after five other kids. Winners who chose Sugar Daddies weren't stupid. They might have opted for Sugar Babies instead, the bite-sized caramel-flavored jellybeans. Sugar Babies could easily have been shared. However, with a Sugar Daddy, winner took all!

Paul never celebrated a win with us. Instead, he was furious that he had to give up a nickel candy bar for a penny win, not considering that we had likely spent at least ten cents trying to win the five-cent candy bar. But Halloween was the day of the year that made Paul angriest, with the throngs of neighborhood kids who all lived along Florida Street or many of the streets branching off Florida. We'd congregate around Paul's in our costumes on the holiday until darkness descended, mostly for a chance to get him back for yelling at us all year. We'd go in, a few at a time, but a large pack of trick-or-treaters would stand waiting outside for their turn to bother Paul. We'd pretend that we didn't see his sign that read, "No Free Candy for Any Reason," and we'd go in, approach the counter, and shout, "Trick or treat." Rather than pretending to be the tiniest bit tolerant with the children of his neighborhood clientele, Paul would become further enraged with each new group that came in teasing for candy. We never really expected any free candy from Paul, but it was our one chance each year to retaliate for him calling us meshugenahs. Why we didn't think to respond with the annoying childhood reply, "I know you are, but what am I?" still irks me!

20

My Hideaway

Looking directly at the house on 55 Edwin Street, one still sees two doors on the front porch. The one on the right has the address of 53 Edwin Street. The recessed door on the left side of the front porch is 55 Edwin Street. An additional, small, third-floor attic apartment can only be accessed from the inside back hall stairs or the outside back porch steps. It is also 55 Edwin Street. Because of the size of the uppermost living quarters, the house was called neither a double-decker or triple-decker, or even a two-story or three-story house. Instead, it was officially a two-and a-half-story house.

When my family passed papers (took official ownership of their very first home when I was ten years old), we had a grand celebration. It was the first time ever that we were allowed to get take-out food from the McDonald's Restaurant on the corner of Gallivan Boulevard and Granite Street. This was so long ago that it still had the original Golden Arches on the structure.

My parents had noticed when they viewed their house with the realtor that the third-floor apartment was in abysmal shape. The small front balcony (still on the house today) was packed from floor to ceiling with old newspapers layered with pigeon droppings. Wearing gloves, my mother and I spent at least a full week emptying the balcony of mounds of soaked and smelly newspapers. For another full week, we scrubbed and scrubbed. I have hardly worked as hard since, but we left it gleaming.

The rest of the little place had been poorly cared for, too. Kathy and I helped scrape wallpaper, and scrubbed walls and floors in preparation for my parents to paint, hang new wallpaper, and put new linoleum down on the floors. It was a homey abode by the time we were finished. A young couple expecting their first child moved into the apartment. Prior to the birth of their baby, both the husband and wife worked full-time during the days, so we never got to know them very well.

Whereas my father often had night school classes, my mother and I frequently had tea in the kitchen in the evening before I went to bed. One night the baby was coming, its parents were at the hospital, and the apartment was empty. Or so we thought. We heard a scuffle from upstairs and went to the kitchen door because it opened out onto the back hallway. Hearing more noise from the attic apartment, we went out into the landing to listen more carefully. When the noise suddenly abated, we went back inside, thinking no more about the incident than that we had misheard something.

The next day, the husband came to our back door to announce the birth of their healthy baby. He then inquired whether we had heard anything unusual the previous evening. We described what we had heard but explained that because there had been no commotion or anything to suggest a disturbance, we'd thought no more of it. He responded that the apartment had been broken into and robbed while they were gone! There had been an actual breaking and entering in our home, and we could easily have interrupted the perpetrators when we went out into the hallway. The husband told us the couple collected precious coins and had brought home from their safety deposit box much of their valuable stash to cash in for baby furniture, but now it was all gone. Shortly after they returned with their new baby, they moved in with family members who could help to cushion them after the financial loss and provide baby care when the couple both returned to work.

In general, because of its small size, tenant stays in the attic apartment tended to be brief. This was a good learning experience for my parents, as they continued to rent out various floors of the house over the next few years.

But my favorite part of the building was in our second-floor apartment, the largest unit. A set of stairs led from the front porch up to the second floor. The front porch entrance had a heavy wooden door which locked, and a glass-paned door at the top of the stairs, which stairs led into our apartment. This set of stairs were my not-so-secret hideaway—my reading room and escape place. I spent many hours, particularly on rainy weekends, sequestered on a large corner landing. I had room on the landing for a bit of comfortable spreading-out, and would hold my book in my arms, or prop it on the step above. A bright light above my head illuminated the hallway sufficiently for reading. And the stairs above me made convenient shelves for a snack and a drink.

I was allowed to do my reading in my hideaway unless there were chores to be done. It was a rare event when I was allowed to read at leisure, typically being called to feed or change a baby, or set the table for supper, destroying my quiet reverie. One midweek afternoon, I was sneaking in some reading before it was time to help cook supper. I was happily ensconced when Kathy called me in. As I came in, she dashed down the steps, thinking that I had cached something belonging to her in my hideaway. I got angry and locked the chain on our glass-paned front door to keep her from getting back into our apartment from the stairway. She banged and banged on the panes, demanding I open the door. My mother intervened, reminding us that supper needed to be on the table when Dad came in at 4:15 p.m. It was after four already and since this was law in our house, Kathy and I both knew we were cruising for a bruising.

Kathy had pushed open the door into the apartment as much as the chain lock would allow. I assured everyone that I was letting her in, but Kathy was in a rage. As I pushed closed the door so I could release the chain, Kathy brandished a fist and made a threatening "punching" gesture. Our timing was disastrous. The moment Dad was coming in the back door, Kathy and I made a pane of glass shatter.

The rest of the law about my father's daily homecoming from work was being all in our places with bright shiny faces, ready to help ourselves to food after my mother served my father his supper. It was a near-sacred sequence. No one was *ever* supposed to upset my father when he came home. He had done a hard day's work and we were to recognize and honor that—clean, quiet, and in our seats while he washed his hands, removed his outer work shirt, and sat at the head of his table.

Arriving home to shattering glass and two girls screaming was not part of the scenario. He roared, *"What the hell is going on?"* My mother was upset, babies were crying. Jeanie and little Lonnie were fussing for their supper. Things were not going to end well.

Within ten minutes, Kathy and I had swept up and safely disposed of the glass. We made arrangements with my father as to how we would both earn the money to replace the glass. We would go to the hardware to get the supplies after school the next day. It would have been that night if Kathy and I could have walked to Orbit's together—no car rides for us. We had caused the problem. We were fully responsible for making things right. But babies needed to be fed, changed, and put to bed, and we had dishes and homework to do, so our father had to make do with an hour of lecturing us as we did our chores. The next day we assisted him in the replacement of the window. I was finally happy: My hideaway was restored and once again, I could read in relative solitude.

21

The Enabler

Admittedly, I have always been one of those people. I thought it was just being nice. I have a long history of being that someone who rightfully gets blamed when others are caught with goodies they've been otherwise prohibited.

This history started with Mum. No one ever forbade her to have the beautiful Hummels like the many she admired in Aunt Priscilla's collection. But my mother was modest in her wishes and resisted the very slight temptation to use any of our limited household money to buy herself a gift. She managed to scrimp and save, and to provide everything we needed and more. But I had noticed the slight look of envy on my mother's face when we visited Aunt Priscilla, cousins Rita, Mary, and Julia, and their Hummel statuettes—all around the living room.

Hummels are porcelain figurines based on the drawings of Sister Maria Innocentia Hummel. Porcelain maker Franz Goebel commercialized Sister Hummel's drawings from 1930s Germany and Switzerland, and American soldiers started purchasing them and bringing them home as souvenirs. Hummels' popularity in the United States grew through the 1970s, and though it has waned, Hummel figurines remain a desirable gift.

So, Mum loved Hummels but would never buy them for herself. On my way to Saint Mark's School and Church, I walked past a Dorchester Avenue gift shop each day that always had a small supply of Hummels. Sometimes, I would stop in and browse. I took particular interest in the Hummels display cabinet as Mum had hinted to me about one small three-piece set in particular.

I sneaked into the gift shop one Saturday afternoon on the way home from confession and purchased the three statuettes with babysitting money I had saved. I was gleeful bringing them home, hiding them, and anticipating the look on her face when I gave them to her on Mother's Day, months away.

It turns out Mum was also sneaky. As she put away our laundry, she always took a peek to see what else we might have secreted in our bureau drawers. I wasn't very talented at concealing anything. She found the three little Hummels, in the bag emblazoned with the name of the gift shop.

Mum wanted them—immediately. When I got home from school that day, she offhandedly reiterated how much she really loved Aunt Priscilla's Hummels. I feigned disinterest. Mum then said, not so timidly, that she had seen a bag in my bureau drawer from the local gift shop. Again, I ignored her hint. Frustrated, she said, "You bought my Hummels, didn't you?" I couldn't lie to her and I sheepishly admitted that I did have them, but that they were for her for Mother's Day.

It was at this point that my mother did almost the worst thing she has ever done to me. She looked at me forlornly, and said quietly, "Mother's Day isn't for months. If I died before that time, I would never have gotten to enjoy them."

I was flabbergasted. Not only had she tricked me into giving her the gift prematurely—I was shocked she would resort to such a tactic to get what she wanted. I ran to the bureau drawer, grabbed the bag of Hummels, and gave them to her. She was tickled pink, and yes, I had just become an enabler.

The worst part is that the trauma seems to have planted that fatalistic idea into my head. Now, if I buy someone a gift early and attempt to keep it until the event, the remote possibility of a premature, deadly event for the intended recipient haunts me. Thus, I have never been able to hold back on giving people gifts the moment I have them in my possession.

While recently watching a Kirwan family video from 1960 with me, my husband saw what might have been interpreted as an excess of presents for the then four children. The house was decorated beautifully, the picture completed by the adorable black and white kitten scampering around the room. We looked like the ideal middle-class family. My husband said, "I thought your father lectured you constantly about privilege, and informed you, to your shock, that your family was lower middle-class." I responded that he was correct, but my father also fundamentally believed we could achieve whatever goals we set in life, including that of desired social class, based on the amount of education that we acquired.

I told my husband that we, likewise, shared my father's contention that education began at home. It had been my father's self-designated role to conduct our family's "civics for suppah" lessons. From the time we were old enough to sit at the kitchen table and express our thoughts, we were expected by my father to speak with intelligence and clarity. For him, that included appropriate grammar (one might even be challenged to spell a word to ensure the right form was being used), and proper manners (for instance: No elbows on the table). My father, in particular, was extremely well-versed in politics. The onus fell on each of us to be able to participate in, or at least listen actively to, impassioned arguments about the state of affairs of Boston, the nation, and the world. My father and mother were both voracious readers, demonstrating to us that education in itself, whether formal or informal, was of immeasurable value.

Because a number of my friends took Irish step dancing, whereas we took ballet, jazz, and tap at Barbara DeVoe's School of Dance, I asked my mother if I could take Irish step lessons which I preferred. My mother's immediate response was, "We are not Irish. We are American." I was very confused. I pointed out to my mother we had Irish surnames on both sides, and that most of our friends and family claimed Irish ancestry. My argument was that we must be Irish, since Kirwans were one of the original Fourteen Tribes of Galway. But none of this carried weight with my mother. Had either of us known I would marry a Boston-born Lebanese man whose last name happened to be Kelley she would have felt vindicated that we weren't truly Irish. But at that point, despite all evidence to the contrary, my mother continued denying our heritage. As well, she could not be faulted for making me the enabler that I am. She believed strongly that sacrifice strengthened one's character. So, my childhood Irish step dance lessons never came to be. But at age 58, I took *sean nos* (an old-style, traditional solo form of Irish dance) at the Irish Cultural Center in Canton. I also learned to get what I wanted for myself, even if it took a while.

My mother's denial of our Irish heritage was not uncommon at the time. For many decades, the goal in the United States for immigrants and their descendants was assimilation—to become a part of the patchwork quilt of nationalities that make up America. I didn't argue the point initially, but a few years later I asked again if I could take Irish step dancing lessons. Her response was "Irish step dancing is a bunch of stiff-armed clodhoppers." Despite that interesting classification, I still wanted to be one. But my mother was not an enabler. No matter how badly I wanted Irish step dancing lessons, she never gave in to my pleas.

Our socioeconomic status was a part of our frequent discussion of aspects of our life in Dorchester. It was our civic responsibility to understand the economy, our place in it, and how that translated to future plans. My parents were self-sacrificing and expected we would be too. They spent little money on themselves, and truly made sure that their children had everything they needed. They were also both very ambitious and they advocated self-sacrifice where necessary to achieve desired goals. Personal rewards were to be earned, not expected. While I agree, in essence, I have always found much joy in giving, which can be considered by some to be enabling. I am guilty as charged, yet not regretful.

As one might imagine, with seven children, my mother was often "expecting." (She used the modest terminology because she couldn't bring her bashful self to say the explicit word "pregnant.") During her pregnancies, she suffered from high blood pressure, varicose veins, and long-term morning sickness. With at least one pregnancy, she endured toxemia. But during all of them, she craved foods forbidden by her obstetricians.

Pregnancy cravings don't necessarily respond to reason. Mum still wanted the prohibited snacks. Knowing that I would, in my childish innocence, satisfy her gastronomic desires, and not reveal her prohibited snack attacks, I would eagerly run to the corner store to buy her favorite pickles and pepperoncinis. The excessive sodium the treats contained was a potential contributor to the dangerously high blood pressure associated with toxemia, yet she couldn't resist. While she beamed with satisfaction while savoring the craved saltiness, I would keep a watchful eye out for anyone who might rat her out to Dad. I would then stash the wrappers in the "ash can" (trash barrel, in Dorchester parlance) to foil detection by anyone who might be monitoring her pregnancy diet. Despite our sneaking around together to satisfy her salt cravings, my mother gave birth in December of 1964 to a healthy baby girl, the fifth of seven kids.

The stories of my enabling are numerous, and yet I feel no shame.

My father had suffered his first myocardial infarction (heart attack) at age 49. Despite his newly diagnosed cardiac disease, Dad resisted every attempt by his cardiologist to get him to follow a heart-healthy diet and cardiac rehab exercise programs. Since his first cardiac event was rather mild compared to the cardiac muscle damage he sustained from subsequent myocardial infarctions, my father felt healthy and only slightly frightened after his first incident.

He had been an occasional jogger for years, usually getting the impetus to run within a few days of engaging in a gastronomic feast and the subsequent belly discomfort. Once while ruminating about a recent overindulgence, my father spontaneously got off the couch and went out for a run. Within two hours, we all got notifications that my father was in the Emergency Room at Jordan Hospital. After it was determined that he had, in fact, suffered a heart attack, he was kept in the coronary care unit.

We were advised to let him rest quietly, with only my mother allowed to visit for the first few days. After that, we could each visit as he allowed. The healthcare staff had the final say over the number of visitors and the time each could spend, but my father got to decide who was allowed and when. He called me days after the initial event and asked me to come in early that afternoon. I did what he asked. While I was visiting, he emphasized to me how good he felt, and that he would have no restrictions. I was working as a Registered Nurse at another hospital at the time, and I doubtfully repeated, "No restrictions?"

"None!" he answered. "In fact, I want you to go get me a Chinese luncheon special, two beers, and a package of cigars right now."

"Dad!" I gasped, "Are you kidding me?" He got enraged and his eyes began to bulge as his face turned nearly purple. "*I told you what I want! I am in a private room and my personal cardiologist said I have no restrictions!"*

Again, I doubted him, but honestly feared that his rage was about to trigger another heart attack. Against my better judgment, I hastily beat my retreat, and came back within an hour with the items he had demanded.

I have to admit that he looked at me with what looked like pure love as he bit into the egg rolls, swigged the beer straight from the bottles, and then lit up a stogie and puffed away happily. The cardiac care unit was an old traditional single-room floor, with no central nursing station for close visual monitoring of patients. Further, he had insisted that I shut his door. In full disclosure, I must say that smoking was still allowed in private rooms in most hospitals at the time, but this was a cardiac unit.

Suddenly the door flew open and in rushed a near-crazed cardiologist. *"Mister Kirwan!"* Dr. Abernathy shouted, "What the hell are you doing? You just had a myocardial infarction."

Without flinching at his own dishonesty, my father looked at the physician and calmly said, "Blame my daughter." He pointed his finger directly at me and said, "She brought all of this in to me! She should know better. She's a nurse."

There it was. He had thrown me right under the bus. I knew better than to protest, so I had to sit quietly, allowing myself to be subjected to a vicious, but deserved, tongue-lashing by the enraged cardiologist. I said not a word in my own defense. I looked over at my father, and he was smiling smugly, having escaped the justified outburst of his doctor. As for me, I knew it was wrong to have honored my father's wishes, but what can I say? I am an enabler.

Oh, and then there was the time my somewhat depressed teenage daughter told me she'd "feel so much better if we could just go to Puerto Rico. I've always wanted to go," and I came home with five airline tickets and a hotel booking at the Wyndham El Conquistador.

And there was the daughter who wanted her wedding ceremony and reception at the Wedding Pavilion in Disneyworld. . . .

And the daughter who can't get enough Disney Adventures. . . . Yep, she's always happy, too.

And the six grandchildren. . . .

The lesson learned is that it is easier for me to say "yes" than "no," and it is a hell of a lot more expensive as well. But enabling makes me happy, and my happiness makes my husband happy. So the label is justified. I am an enabler. I will also be working till the day of my funeral. Enabling is expensive!

22

⟋⟋

Diddling, Dinks, and Tiddlywinks

As the second oldest child in a big family, I was always called upon to take care of neighborhood kids as well as my own younger siblings. That was just how it was. Although the phrase "it takes a village" did not become common in America till many decades later, it was a fact of life in large, Dorchester Irish families. If there was a mother or child in need of assistance, the older neighborhood girls would be summoned. We were most often outside watching our own little siblings anyway. Another kid or two to watch was just a way of life. When I was sent to any one of the local neighborhood stores to do errands for my mother, neighbors would add their needed items to my list, and send a couple of their little ones to accompany me.

One family in our neighborhood was Polish. Although I had a Polish uncle, this ethnic group was relatively uncommon in Dorchester; the Poles lived mostly in South Boston. But on Edwin Street, we had the Nowaks. Mrs. Nowak spent a lot of time outside of her house. I could spot her from my front yard, with her unkempt, bleached blond hair, her raggedy housedress, and the ever-present lit cigarette dangling from her lips. On spotting me, she'd yell up the street, "Judy, c'mere! I need ya help!" Frequently it was just to watch her likewise platinum-tressed offspring as they played on the sidewalks. Other times she would summon me into her apartment to monitor the kids while she watched television.

Mr. Nowak worked odd hours, nothing like my own father's punctually leaving the house at 6:45 a.m. and returning home exactly at 4:15 p.m. Mr. Nowak was often home during the day, which made me uncomfortable when I was in their house. He was also usually dirty and seemed to spend most of the time sprawled on the couch with a jelly jar of vodka. I wasn't very familiar with the effects of alcohol yet, but I did notice him acting sloppier and sloppier, if possible, the more drinks he consumed.

I don't know for sure if Mrs. Nowak was drinking the same clear liquid out of her teacup, but her speech got strangely slurred as she sipped that "tea." Her language was always inappropriate, but she spoke to me, a fifth-grader, as if I was her age. She said her husband was "diddling the teenage babysitter." I had no idea what that meant. She continued, "If I catch him screwing her, I am going to shove his cock down his throat." Naïve as the day I was born, I didn't understand what a rooster had to do with carpentry. She cackled when she saw my puzzled expression. I knew enough not to ask for clarification, but I also intuitively recognized that I should not ever be in that apartment again.

I never spoke of my discomfort to my parents; it just felt wrong to be around the Nowaks. Having been so sheltered was not always a bonus. The Nowaks were deviant, *that* I realized. What was particularly confusing to me was that they let their kids play with food—specifically hot dogs, and that the kids (a boy my age and three younger siblings) were frequently naked as they ran around the house. Bobby and his brother would chase his two sisters, all of them unclothed, through the halls and bedrooms, as their mother chortled. Bobby brandished an uncooked frankfurter, laughingly threatening to "put it up the girls." The girls dangled their own raw hot dogs in front of their pelvises and mimicked their older brother's swinging appendage. Their gross parents would laugh.

I was terribly worried about what my parents would have thought about the waste of good food. But I never told them. After a while, I caught on that something in the Nowak household was seriously awry and learned to feign deafness when Mrs. Nowak yelled my name from down the street.

Next door to our house lived another large family. My friend Joanie, in sixth grade with me, had just succeeded Patrick Donnelly as my best friend. Joanie and I spent many happy hours together, often sitting on my front steps with needles, scissors, and fabric, crafting our very own beach bags. We gathered rope from our cellar and cobbled together straps long enough to throw over our shoulders for ferrying all of our necessary artifacts on afternoons at Malibu Beach. We made enough beach bags that we eventually sold them for two dollars each in the neighborhood. (Anything to earn some cash, especially if it was something we enjoyed doing. Babysitting for neighbors and relatives was a lucrative source of income, even though it only netted me fifty cents per hour. It was great. I loved little kids. I had to babysit at home all the time for free, and the fairly frequent babysitting jobs paid me to both get out of the house and to make money.)

It was often difficult to escape to the beach without having Joanie's twin brother following on our heels, mooning after an unsuspecting me. It was also rare for us to escape from our homes unsaddled with younger siblings. But the event did occur every now and then. On one of these hot summer days, we packed our new satchels with towels, Coppertone suntan lotion, and our transistor radios.

We strolled down Edwin Street to Adams Street, crossed over to Victory Road, and proceeded to Morrissey Boulevard. If the bridge over the beach was closed, allowing foot and vehicle traffic to pass, we'd quickly complete the nearly two-and-a-half mile journey to Malibu, and choose a spot on the hot sand to lounge till we blistered our fair skin. If the bridge was open to allow larger boats to go through, our trip either to the beach or home could be significantly delayed until it closed again. (The bridge seemed to open unexpectedly much more often when we were rushing home in time for supper.)

Once on the beach, we'd spread out our towels, tune in to Arnie "Woo Woo" Ginsburg, the popular Boston talk show host on WMEX. His tag lines included "Good guys a-go-go"; this was the place on the dial where "the hits keep on coming." Our goals were simply to listen to rock and roll while hoping, in vain, to achieve a bronzy tan. WMEX addressed our direct concerns (intended for beachgoers such as us) by announcing on the half-hour, "turn so you don't burn." Coppertone lotion, applied liberally, was expected to protect us from our scorching exposure to the harsh summer sun. Instead, I spent a fair amount of my allowance on Noxzema skin cream, intended to quell the excruciating pain of skin burned to a crisp by those damaging UV rays. A tan was never in the cards for this blue-eyed, blond Irish-American girl.

Unlike the better known California beach, our Malibu was wedged on a little spit between Morrissey Boulevard and the Southeast Expressway. It was small enough that we could walk the periphery and quickly be on the opposite side's Savin Hill Beach. On days when the tide was low, even poor swimmers could paddle across from Malibu Beach to Savin Hill.

On the beach, we had everything that a city kid could want. We had sun, sand, saltwater, a snack bar, showers, and restrooms. For a young Catholic girl with hormones beginning their ascent, we had even more than we could dream of . . . a place where one could actually see bare skin on teenage boys and not have to confess it to Father McCarthy on Saturday. We didn't know a lot about those male bodies, just that they made us feel tingly to look at them. Because we had brothers, we knew the basic parts. As Catholic pre-teens, we didn't have a clue as to what the private parts were called or what they were used for. And I mean the private parts of males *or* females.

In school and at home, modesty of mind and body was an inviolable rule. We learned in religion class that "marital activity" (never defined or discussed) was only for purposes of procreation. A Catholic school injunction forever burned in my brain: When married men come home from work and find their wives scrubbing dishes they immediately begin to kiss and cuddle the back of their wives' necks. This was a problem because? "As a couple joined in the eyes of God, a brief kiss on the cheek from husband to wife is acceptable, but prolonged embrace will lead to sin!"

We were well aware that non-Catholics chuckled at the myth that Catholic girls were prohibited from wearing patent leather shoes because the shine would reflect their underpants to the sex always tempted by Satan. Another amusing myth was that Catholic kids attending Catholic dances were instructed by chaperoning nuns to "leave room for the Holy Ghost," as they inserted their habit-draped arms or yardsticks between couples slow-dancing. But neither of these are myths. They are formal instructions.

One more thing: The only ejaculations that Catholic school-children were ever told about were excited language utterances, such as "Glory be to God!" or "Jesus, Mary, and Joseph!" These ejaculations produced not children, but plenary indulgences, or credits toward heaven. I misunderstood the term "plenary indulgences" to mean "plenty of indulgences" and that sounded like a good thing to me. Since even silent ejaculations counted, I spent hours of otherwise idle time silently announcing my praise toward the heavens.

Finally, we might have changed diapers of baby brothers and sisters, but we never really looked at the anatomical elements or learned their names. We became proficient with a wet rag, knew to rinse a poopy diaper in the toilet before putting it into the diaper pail, and how to swaddle the baby in clean cotton cloth. The two big concerns were not to stick the baby with the diaper pins, and to drape baby boys' private parts with a clean diaper while changing them to avoid ending up with a face full of tinkle. Joanie and I intuited that there was something mysterious and forbidden about private parts, but we didn't have a clue about the motivation to exploit innocent young girls that existed in our protected world.

On the day at Malibu Beach that Joanie and I got a clue about just how sheltered we had been, we had found a spot, not too far from the water. We anchored our towels with rocks, slathered each other with Coppertone, and settled down for an afternoon of sunning, snacking, and swimming. Shortly after we positioned ourselves for the greatest amount of sun exposure, an overweight old man dragged his webbed beach chair near our towels. We glanced at each other, curious, but silently agreed he wasn't a bother.

He pushed his chair onto the corner of Joanie's towel, and began to ramble about nothing of any consequence. As Joanie and I sat upright on our towels, staring up to listen to him, our eyeballs were level with his private parts. His legs were spread as he nattered on, and he'd occasionally grab his crotch, adjusting his anatomy. No matter how humiliated we increasingly felt, we couldn't avoid seeing his bits and pieces. As well-mannered though naïve girls, we continued to engage in polite, if extremely strained, conversation. He maintained steady eye contact with the two of us, now writhing with discomfort. As he continued to touch the front of his swim trunks, a pink, puffy mound appeared at his groin, about two feet in front of our eyes.

Once again, having been raised Catholic and generally deferential, we didn't get up and kick the crap out of this pervert. Instead, we decided independently that it would be rude to assume any nasty intent, and just to bring this conversation to a respectful close. We stood up, folded our towels and packed up our checkered beach bags. We bade him well (again, as nice Catholic girls) and told him that we needed to be home in time for supper.

As we walked back across the bridge on Morrissey Boulevard, we timidly questioned what had happened to us. Approaching Victory Road, I asked Joanie, "Did anything seem weird to you about that guy?" Joanie answered tentatively, "Umm. . . . There was something soft and pink sticking outside of his swim trunks." "Do you think it was a marshmallow?" I asked. Joanie, with more brothers than I had, answered, "I think it was his dink!!"

We both shrieked as we continued walking. "That is disgusting!" I asked Joanie, "Do you think he did this to us on purpose?" She nodded sagely. We both felt really dirty but agreed that we shouldn't tell anyone about what had happened. Decades later, I still fantasize about going back and shooting the pervert, right in his mushy little marshmallow. So much for the polite Catholic girl!

And yet as we talked, we became aware that inappropriate behavior of this sort was far more common than we were taught at home or at school. I realized that the beach episode made me feel the way I had after an event at the home of my former friend Debbie from Saint Ambrose School—like scrubbing my skin with steel wool.

As I said, my mother gave birth to seven children, but never said the word "pregnant." She and others carrying yet-to-be-born babies were always "expecting." If we had to use the toilet as young kids, we said we had to "tinkle," or "wee-wee." As we got older, the only adequate reason for addressing elimination at all was when the one bathroom was occupied by my father each morning, with four kids lined up outside the door, moaning and clenching relevant muscles as we waited our turn. We couldn't say "poop." We needed to "have a bowel movement." (Admittedly, one of us would occasionally confuse our consonants and state that we had to have a "vowel" movement. Yes, we were rapidly corrected.) Decorum also demanded we say that we had to "urinate" instead of less polite references to liquid elimination.

I had on rare occasions in other homes experienced a different type of language and attitude regarding various body processes. But protected as we were, I never fully understood unacceptable behavior when it came to invasions of privacy in word or deed.

While attending Saint Ambrose, I had become friends with Debbie, a girl who lived in a third-floor apartment on Adams Street directly across from the Mary Hemenway School, which she attended. As fourth-graders, we were often allowed to play at each other's apartments. The assumption was that if there were parents at home, the kids would be well-supervised and protected. This turned out to be false when it came to Debbie's house. Parenting in this home was negligible at best, and language used in front of and to children was inappropriate and confusing.

I got an inkling things were different at Debbie's one day when her mother startled me in the bathroom, where I was washing my hands. The door was closed, yet Mrs. Rosetti barged in. To my shock, she lifted her housedress, dropped her underwear and plunked her plump bottom onto the toilet seat. She spread her knees apart and announced to me, "I gotta pee. Is that okay?" I didn't have an answer, but I quickly escaped into the hallway. Scarlet with humiliation, I stood silently and took a series of deep breaths until I could calm down before joining Debbie to read together in the parlor. Sitting side by side on a couch with our books, we were also tasked with watching the younger Rosettis.

The doorbell rang, but before anyone answered it, Debbie's maternal uncle, a loud, blustery man, lurched up the stairs and entered the apartment. He and Mrs. Rosetti kicked us out of the front room, lit up cigarettes, and shared a couple of beers. Debbie and I moved into the kitchen. After a while, we heard raucous laughter coming from the parlor. Debbie, whom my mother called "a pushy girl," ran back into the parlor and demanded, "What are you laughing at?"

Standing behind Debbie I could see that both adults were leering out the front window toward the Hemenway playground. There was something about their laughter that made my skin crawl, but I had no idea why. Debbie persisted in asking what they saw across the street. More disgusting guffawing came from her mother and uncle, but no explanation. In exasperation, Debbie yelled, "Why are you watching those people? What are they doing?" Mrs. Rosetti spat back, "Well, they ain't playin' tiddlywinks!"

I was horrified! Tiddlywinks in the playground? I had played tiddlywinks a number of times with my siblings, but never felt squeamish the way I did now. I was supposed to stay for dinner, but shakily made an excuse about needing to be home early. I trembled all the way home and decided not to tell my parents what had happened. I wanted Debbie as a friend, and I knew that if I said anything, our playtimes together would be prohibited. Ultimately, I did admit to my mother that Debbie's mother had come in and urinated in front of me. As expected, I was banned from Debbie's home by my parents. I was so relieved. But I never, ever played tiddlywinks again.

23

⚜

The Loss of Innocence

Like most Dorchester neighborhoods of my youth, we were overrun with kids. Many lived on Edwin Street, as we did. Others were friends, neighbors, and relatives visiting those who lived on our street. Kids were in and out of each other's houses, and it was often confusing, even to the parents, which kids belonged to whom.

One morning my sister Jeanie was at the neighbors' down the street, the O'Connors. In addition to their own children, the O'Connors had a young niece, Maureen, staying for the day. Maureen and her cousin Erin were playing with my sister Jeanie. After being down the street only a short time, Jeanie scurried home, sobbing and shaking. She kept repeating to my mother, "Mrs. O'Connor is in her kitchen. She was on the telephone crying and crying." Jeanie had no explanation for Mrs. O'Connor's hysteria but said that when the neighbor had hung up the phone, Mrs. O'Connor covered her tear-stained face with both hands and was unable to speak to anyone, much less give the children an explanation of whatever had happened.

My sister Kathy was a few years older than the O'Connor children, and spent hours helping around their apartment or babysitting. Kathy went to their apartment to see if things were as Jeanie had described. Kathy quickly returned home to tell us that she had heard someone say that visiting cousin Maureen's two little brothers were dead. Kathy didn't know why people were saying that, and no one knew at that point if the tragic information was accurate. Rumors, rather than fact, were the order of the day, with the entire O'Connor family simply trying to cope with what only they knew to have happened.

A *Boston Globe* article the next day confirmed that an investigation was underway in the deaths of two little boys, possibly from an overdose of sleeping pills, in a different Dorchester apartment the previous afternoon. The bodies of the children, Brendan O'Connor, five years old, and Brian O'Connor, two years old, had been discovered in their home by their father, Brendan O'Connor, Sr. on his return from work. O'Connor found his wife Susan unconscious in another room. She was taken immediately to Carney Hospital where her name was put on the danger list. She was determined to have suffered from an overdose of sleeping pills. Police had found her suicide note that read, "I can't stand it anymore. This is the best way out." Two empty bottles of sleeping pills were found. The note from Susan to her husband continued, begging for forgiveness, and asking him to take care of their daughter Maureen, who was with our neighbors at the time of her brothers' deaths. Autopsies revealed that the boys had been suffocated. Within months of their deaths, 25-year-old Susan O'Connor was indicted by the Suffolk County Grand Jury on two counts of manslaughter.

I have never forgotten about the sudden deaths of the two little boys with whom we played. In our circle of family and friends, the old-fashioned phrase "little pitchers have big ears" was oft-repeated. This was to indicate to speakers that anything that they said in front of children would be heard and considered carefully. So instead, there were always secrets and conversations that were cut off abruptly if children were present. Although no one in my life ever again discussed the deaths of young Brendan and Brian, they were forgotten by some, and acutely remembered by others. What I remember most, more than specific characteristics of the children, was the constant secrecy. If I asked my mother or anyone else direct questions about what happened to the boys, such as was their mother okay? Who took care of their sister Maureen if the mother hadn't survived? I was told only that it was "none of my business." This represented to me that the truth would not always be told. In my mind, children could mysteriously die. Adults could disappear. News stories would be forgotten or ignored. I became worried . . . afraid of what else might happen or have happened in my life that I was not informed about. How could one ever be certain about anything in life if information was hidden. Were there more children who mysteriously died that I never knew about? Had adults from my life just disappeared? The answer, I found out in time, was that yes, not everything is, or should necessarily be, revealed to innocent children. For while the truth shall set you free, it can also enslave you. I understand as a parent why young children are not always told the brutal truth. But in trying to protect the innocence of children, uncertainty and anxiety about the unknown can take its place.

My questions about the O'Connor family stayed with me until recent years, when a serendipitous finding resolved this particular troubling question for me. I had tried for so many years to understand what had happened to the children, and their surviving family members. Even while teaching Boston police officers, I prevailed upon a female detective who became a friend of mine, asking if she could help me find information in the Boston Police archives. She spoke with the archivist and was told only that the records "could not be located." The detective added to me that it was fairly likely that someone in the family was connected enough to the police department to have had the records buried, especially since so many years had elapsed since the incident.

A serendipitous event led me down the path to the answers. As an ardent *Boston Globe* newspaper reader and archival researcher, I recently discovered that the *Globe's* print articles are available online as far back as the late 1800s. But it was a fortuitous discovery while reading years ago, rather than discerning research, that pointed me to an article during the Christmas season many years after the triple tragedy. An article in December of 2006 described an event featuring *Globe* Santa and his helpers collecting money for the traditional mission of the Christmas season. Pictured with the article was a two-year-old local girl in her Christmas finery giving *Globe* Santa some chocolate candy before she placed the coins held in her little fist into the donation bin.

The article described an older father with his adult daughter—Brendan O'Connor and Maureen O'Connor West, who had stopped to watch the captivating little girl making her donation to *Globe* Santa. Maureen O'Connor West commented to the correspondent that she had been employed at a Boston hospital for many years, and had seen what impoverished families went through, thus she and her father made yearly donations to *Globe* Santa to alleviate the suffering of others.

24

White Gloves and Patent Leather Shoes

Kathy (at age 12) was the first recipient of a grand gift by my parents: a day off from four siblings, including newborn Christine, and being taken in her Sunday best to see *My Fair Lady*, starring Audrey Hepburn. Kathy, always the well-behaved child, was clad in a maroon plaid skirt and color-coordinated sweater, lace-trimmed white socks, the requisite shiny footwear, with her hair done in pin curls. All enjoyed the show, as I was told.

The lofty, yet truthfully overwhelming, plan to hire a babysitter and take each child on a special occasion trip as an "only" worked out just for the first two of us. A year later, I was more than delighted to have my turn at this "white gloves and patent leather shoes" event, when my parents took me to see the movie *The Sound of Music* starring Julie Andrews. These occasions meant more to us than our parents would ever know. Apparently, they held a different kind of memory for Mum and Dad.

That might have been because my experience at the big screen was appropriately Julie Andrews as a misbehaving governess/novice nun trying to decide her true path in life. At one point, I heard my parents singing along, but they were obviously unfamiliar with the score. I *swore* I heard them singing, "How do you solve a problem like Judy?" rather than "Maria," as Rodgers and Hammerstein had written.

I loved the film with all my heart but was truly enchanted by the free things we got on arrival to the theater. An usher gave me my very own *Playbill*, the glossy publication given at nearly every theater everywhere, that describes the performance, the characters, the players and their biographies, plus advertisements for so many restaurants and products far outside our family's modest budget. But the *Playbills* were free, and I couldn't have been happier.

As I sat to await the start of the show, I discovered a cologne insert tucked into the middle of the Playbill. The advertisement was in a cellophane envelope, which allowed the light citrus scent of *Je Reviens* to be detectable. I was overcome with joy! Not only was this surprise pack *free*, but it smelled better than any cologne I had ever sniffed from some old aunt's wrinkly neck.

The truth of the matter is that I was so enthralled by the event, the discovery, and the cost (none except for the price of three tickets), that I tucked the perfume insert into my patent leather pocketbook. To my awe, when we departed along with the heavy crowd at the end of the show, I found that not everyone had appreciated their gifts as I had. There were *Je Reviens* inserts all over the theater floor, discarded by patrons who had not then (and likely never did) become environmentally aware.

I was aware of *free* only. To my parents' chagrin, rather than departing the show with the deportment of a well-educated parochial school child, I dropped to my knees every 15 seconds or so to sweep the floor with both arms, gathering as many of the discarded *Playbills* as I could carry. Initially I sifted through just for the *Je Reviens* inserts, still wrapped in cellophane to prolong the provocative scent, but as I was being hurried along by occasional kicks on my backside to give up the hoarding and leave with the one *Playbill* that I had been given, I thought, *"Never!"* "Boot my backside all you need to, but I am getting every dropped delight from here till we are on the train home."

At home I counted over 40 of the precious inserts, and secretly bemoaned all those left behind, on the theater floor no less, to be discarded. If only my parents had given me an hour and an empty shopping bag! But it was not to be. In fact, the well-intentioned, "one performance, one child's special day," ended with me. I vaguely recall Jeanie and Little Lonnie together getting bundled off with my parents to see *Batman* in a local theater the following year. They were happy with that. They got candy.

25

Enrichment Without Riches

As was typical for the times, my mother was responsible for our entire household sphere. She took care of everyone and everything inside the house. My father worked full-time and was also responsible for everything outside of the house. Until we were old enough to handle a shovel, he did all of the clearing of the sidewalks in the snow. He filled the furnace with coal and also emptied out the ashes. We recycled the coal ash to render the icy sidewalks less slippery in the winter.

As well, my father worked part-time evenings in addition to his day job and took night school classes at Northeastern. Northeastern was one of the first universities in the nation to provide evening degree programs for adult learners. Recognizing that a significant percentage of their students were married with families, the school put forth extra effort to include those families in the college culture. Each Christmas, Northeastern University would sponsor a production of the "Nutcracker" ballet on campus. Following the production would be a family party, complete with a Santa Claus. The Northeastern staff who sponsored the party would suggest to the parents that they provide a wrapped and tagged gift for their child or children for Santa to present during the party. We were beyond delighted to have Santa call our names, even when some of us were past the age of "believing in Santa."

My mother sometimes also took night school classes at Northeastern University, though less and less as each additional child was born, adding to her workload inside the home. However, during the Christmas season each year, my mother got what must have been a break to her: She worked at the South Postal Annex sorting Christmas mail in the evenings. We kids hated that my mother was gone at night, partially because of my father's lack of cooking ability, and also because he was so impatient. At that time, we were unable to fully understand the difficulty for my parents of virtually never having free time for themselves.

With all they had to do, my parents found the time to let us be children. My parents made the most of opportunities that had small to no fees attached. It might be Franklin Park, with our favorite Children's Zoo. It might be a hike in the Blue Hills Reservation, followed by the immensely satisfying trip post-hike to Bents' Broken Cookie Factory in Milton.

Other common outings included the Science Museum; Boston Public Gardens; Edaville Railroad in Carver, Massachusetts, one of the oldest heritage railroads in the United States; numerous branches of the Boston Public Library; and Longfellow's Wayside Inn. We were frequent audience participants on the "Bozo the Clown" show hosted by Frank Avruch, which was produced at WHDH television station on Morrissey Boulevard in Dorchester, and on the "Big Brother" television program hosted by Bob Emery on WBZ-TV in Boston. As well, we often went to the Ice Capades, a traveling show featuring theatrical ice-skating performances at Boston Garden, and to the "Greatest Show on Earth," the Ringling Brothers Barnum and Bailey Circus.

One of the most exiting days I remember was a double-header. That day, my parents had piled us all into the car and had taken us to Nantasket Beach. We swam for a while, and then we kids, as usual, asked to go into the bathhouse. And just as she always did, my mother forbade us from going into the bathhouse "now or ever." As in so much of our lives, my secretive mother never explained why. She just let us assume that bathhouses were not (ever) an appropriate place to go. However, she would shield each of us with towels one by one, as we brushed off sand and salt and changed into shorts from wet bathing suits.

After our swim, we were taken across the street to Paragon Park, our favorite amusement park. At the time, Paragon's roller coaster was said to be one of the longest in the United States. We rode the merry-go-round with the smaller kids in the family, and the older ones of us persuaded our parents to let us go on the bumper cars. We were convinced to go home by the promise of stopping off at Dairy Queen on Gallivan Boulevard for a cherry-dipped ice cream cone. These were truly the happy days of summer.

When we got home, we took turns bathing, more than one at a time. If the tub held three at once, it meant less expenditure on hot water and soap. But by the time the second group got into the tub, it was somewhat soapy and lukewarm. We never knew, either, if one of the little kids who had been bathed first had forgotten the difference between the tub and a toilet. Staged group bathing was a common event in big families with little spare time or money.

Out of the tub, it was right into pajamas, and then a light supper. But that night, this was all taking place earlier than usual. As we finished washing the dishes, my parents both got amused looks on their faces as they asked each other in front of the four of us, "Is there somewhere we forgot to go?" We were very confused. My parents never seemed to forget a thing—in particular, my frequent misdeeds. But to our shock, we were all directed to go outside and get back into the car. Confused, we kids looked to each other to see if anyone had a hint as to what was going on, but my parents were smiling, so it couldn't be anything bad.

We got into the car and were driving in uncommon silence for just a short period of time when my father pulled into the Neponset Drive-In theater. We would have screamed with excitement if we had been allowed to *be* loud. Instead, we clasped each other's hands and all exclaimed, "We're at the drive-in!" We rode over the angled bumps in the parking area of the theater that held over 1300 cars. My father very carefully chose a spot not far from the concession stands and bathrooms but with little visual obstruction of the screen. We were there, in our pajamas, to watch *Mary Poppins*! We couldn't have been more ecstatic. I peeked in the front seat to see if my mother had managed to sneak a couple of blankets past us. That was another advantage of drive-ins, a "date" for the parents with no babysitting costs, and kids who would snuggle asleep under covers somewhere around intermission time.

As much as I loved the drive-in, I did tend to get bored sitting in the car among wiggling siblings, having to accompany my sisters to the bathroom, and going to the concession stand—normally a privilege. However, as one of the oldest, I was sent often, as people got hungry, thirsty, or felt the twinges of a full bladder. Although I didn't ever have to take Little Lonnie to the bathroom. He always got to "wee wee" in the extra hubcap that we carried inside the car for him.

The movies never started until twilight. By then, younger ones were tired, and often didn't last through much of the movie before taking up most of the room sleeping on the back seat. I would occupy myself during some of these moments by kneeling and looking out the back window to watch the Keystone Camera sign across the highway flash on and off in sequence:

K E Y S T O N E
KEYSTONE
K E Y S T O N E
KEYSTONE

That would amuse me for a short time, and then I might doze off for a while. Evening commuters driving past on the Southeast Expressway could see part of the movie that was playing. That was entertaining for the passengers but could be a dangerous distraction for drivers.

In *Mary Poppins*, as you may remember, Uncle Albert and Bert sing "I Love to Laugh," as they levitate, laughing uncontrollably, to the ceiling, eventually joined by the more tightly wound British nanny Mary Poppins herself. As I dozed fitfully, I kept hearing the song, opening my eyes, then falling asleep again. Woven into my dream was my own being stuck on the ceiling, unable to get down. In my doze, try as I might, I kept rolling over in mid-air, only to hit the ceiling again. I got panicky in my sleep and woke up. As much as I enjoy sleep and would love to be able to float on happy thoughts, I get a feeling of dread on the rare occasions I hear this song, because of that terrifying lack of control that I vividly recall from my dream. Too, I had missed parts of the movie, and that bothered me. So, I headed to the Adams Street branch of the Boston Public Library a few days later to consume the entire book. I was pleased to learn that the laughter was caused by the ingestion of laughing gas by Mary Poppins's Uncle Albert. In the book, they do not use the term in the chemical sense, but to suggest there is a type of intestinal gas that elicits laughter instead of burps.

As I recall each of these places and events, I remain astounded by my parents' devotion to providing all of us with as much enrichment, in both educational and entertainment senses, as they did, with what little discretionary time and money that they had. And best of all, through their influence, my parents' practices of taking advantage of all that Boston and its environs had to offer has become an honored family tradition with our own more financially fortunate offspring.

26

❧

Once in Town . . . The Stores!

A typical day of going into Boston to shop would include a hearty breakfast of hot porridge and milk to fortify ourselves to take on the fray, followed by the essential bathroom stop before leaving home. Next was the brisk walk to the subway, and, once at the destination, to head up the escalator or through the tunnel at Washington Street, depending on which exit you wanted.

The elegant Jordan Marsh was a significant draw for shoppers based on presentation, as well as the quality and quantity of fine products. With many different departments displaying wares from around the world, the store drew shoppers from the many neighborhoods of Boston as well as from the growing "streetcar suburbs."

For the average Boston area family, Christmas season at Jordan Marsh was the major draw of the holidays. Featuring what was originally called "The Enchanted Village of Saint Nicholas," a lavish holiday display was created in 1958. Jordan Marsh Company had commissioned a Bavarian toymaker to create 28 holiday scenes with 250 animated figures. These were prominently positioned in the large front windows encircling Jordan Marsh's Downtown Crossing store throughout the 1960s and into the 1970s. From the windows, the scenes continued on into the store, drawing long lines for the yearly display.

Families came in droves for this event. Another essential element of Christmastime at Jordan Marsh was having an individual or family picture taken with Santa Claus. Santa sat on a velvet upholstered armchair with a large cartouche at the top bearing an "S" for Santa. As the Enchanted Village expanded, it continued from the outside front window displays inside to the sixth floor where the picture with Santa was the final event. To soothe the increasingly impatient children waiting in line, they would be welcomed with a candy cane as they waited to climb on Santa's lap. (My own personal picture with Santa was a particularly meaningful occasion and is contained in this book.)

My parents had lofty plans for their family when they had first one and then a second child. The idea was that each child would be treated as an individual, with special occasions tailored just for them. That worked out well for the first two of us, but as we rapidly became a family with four small children, group activities became the norm.

For purposes of shopping in town throughout the year, like Jordan Marsh, the demographic of Filene's stores was also the well-heeled, and well-paid. Toting bags from Jordan Marsh or Filene's indicated one had sophisticated taste, and an income to match. For our Dorchester family and friends, these "royal" retail establishments were for browsing and aspiring. There were numerous stores that catered to the fiscally average shopper, but for the true bargain shopper, there was no match for Filene's Basement!

The Filene's chain was founded in 1881. The success of the original full-line store in Boston, Massachusetts, was supplemented by the emergence in 1908 of its off-price sister Filene's Basement. Filene's Basement was not just a store, it was an adventure! It was also a frequently visited tourist attraction, as compelling as any other landmark in the Boston city limits but providing more entertainment than most!

The name "Filene's Basement" came from the subterranean location of the discount offshoot of Filene's. Although often mispronounced as "Fill-een's Basement," there was no mistaking that Filene's Basement, off the concourse of the Washington Street MBTA subway stop, despite its lack of windows, was brightly lit and ostentatiously decorated. Their unique Automatic Pricing Policy applied to its surplus merchandise, purchased from other businesses, factory clearances, overstock, and closeout sales goods were marked down on an automatic schedule: A sign outside the Basement promised that items would be reduced by one-quarter after

12 selling days, by one-half after 18 selling days, by three-quarters after 24 selling days, and if unsold thereafter, donated to charity. (The owners estimated that most items sold in no more than 12 days on the sales floor.)

Unlike the refined shopping experience assured by Jordan Marsh and Filenes, Filene's Basement knew its place and its shoppers. We were after "Good Stuff Cheap." Yes, that was a shameless co-optation of the slogan of the now-defunct Building 19 (a closeout and liquidation store that lasted in Boston from 1964 until 2013). Like Filene's Basement, in Building 19, if no one was looking, you'd grab the bargains for yourself!

In fact, Filene's Basement shoppers prided themselves on their graceless and merciless behavior. Once the descent to the Basement had commenced, the primary objectives were to score the highest quality merchandise far below average retail price, starting by rapidly surveying the store and quickly implementing a plan of attack. One had to have rapid reflexes, a strong constitution, and a lack of guilt about tearing a coveted item out of another shopper's hands.

Rules of decorum were all but abandoned in the Basement. In an era where personal modesty and privacy were still sacrosanct, especially for "ladies," most shoppers didn't even bother with dressing rooms. People of all ages, sizes, and conditions peeled off and discarded their own garments at the tables and racks, hastily trying on one item or outfit, stuffing it between their clenched knees if they intended to buy it, or tossing it back onto the pile of still-for-sale goods. Those shoppers with even a hint of body consciousness might duck down between high-heaped counters. Many shoppers shed their clothes only to find that their temporarily discarded jackets, blouses, and sometimes even their bras, had been purchased by another shopper. Others lost their shoes to equally rabid shoppers. Once Cousin Connie went in with her sister Chrissie. Like many others, Chrissie ducked down behind a counter to try on a shirt and placed her own top on a pile of for-sale merchandise. Someone grabbed her (not-for-sale) shirt and dashed to the checkout counter with it. When the salesgirls didn't see a price marked, they'd offer the shopper what seemed fair. Chrissie's shirt was purchased and packaged in a Filene's Basement bag. Chrissie had no other choice than to buy a new blouse to replace the one she had worn into the store.

As much as I dearly loved Filene's Basement and their unbeatable bargains, as a modest Catholic young woman, I could never undress in any store. I even left a Frugal Fannie's (another discount chain) in the 1990s when I found that the dressing room was a virtual communal strip joint. I'm not *that* frugal!

If shoppers had time and money left after exhausting Filene's Basement, and even if their arms were full of bags proclaiming that bargains had been successfully procured, it was tradition for many to head back to Jordan Marsh for one of their famous blueberry muffins. The muffins were known for being oversized, bursting with fresh, ripe blueberries, with a generous sprinkling of sugar on top. The recipe for Jordan Marsh blueberry muffins is still readily available online on multiple sites. However, as accomplished a baker as I am, I have not been able to reproduce the muffins exactly. Or else perhaps my memory has magnified the look and taste of the glorious muffins so that the reality of *my* muffins will never be equal to the satisfaction of the original Jordan Marsh blueberry muffins.

As a Dorchester family, we did not do a lot of shopping in Jordan Marsh. The majority of our clothing was purchased in W. T. Grants in Fields Corner, Orbit's Department Store just off Victory Road on Morrissey Boulevard, and Robert Hall in Codman Square. If our family did go clothes shopping in town, it was to the Filene's Basement, Gilchrist's Basement Store, or the lesser known Raymond's Department Stores, all of which catered to modest family budgets.

In my Dorchester youth, the rare shopping trips where I was alone with my mother brought us midday to the lunch counter at Kresge's where we could purchase three American cold-cut "spuckies" ("spucky" was Boston terminology for a submarine sandwich) for one dollar. With our voracious appetites we happily shared that third bologna and cheese spucky but we had to save some tummy room and any leftover coins for a delightful treat a bit later. Kresge's freezer case showcased our favorite frozen dessert: a slice of harlequin ice cream between two toasted waffles—an ice cream sandwich. So we squeezed in a bit more browsing time in the two-level department store to allow for at least partial digestion of the spuckies. We barely made room in our tummies for the highly anticipated dessert which we consumed just prior to returning to the Washington Street train stop for the return to Ashmont Station in Dorchester and then the walk home. With all that exercise, we were ready to prepare supper together once at home while still savoring lunch.

The Washington Street area was eventually closed to traffic and renamed "Downtown Crossing." Even the train station serving the area was given that appellation. After we moved from Dorchester to South Weymouth, I introduced my new friends to the joys of downtown Boston shopping. Kresge's still made the list of favorite places to go. But as a newly suburban teenager, the primary attraction in Kresge's for us was the photo booth. My friends and I would crowd into the small vault-like structure, try to squeeze two bottoms onto one small round seat, and put fifty cents into the coin slot and pose for pictures. We were very creative in our expressions and gestures captured in the strip of black and white photo paper that came down the outside chute about five minutes after the camera stopped flashing. We most often made silly faces, and I have kept many of these pictures. I have on my piano behind me at the current moment a strip of pictures featuring my friend Barbie. She uncharacteristically made what she thought to be a funny face, and the image instead is of her leering at me. Although posed together for the picture in Kresge's in Boston in 1970, I keep it as potential blackmail literally 50 years later. Yes, it is that much of a threat to her self-image!

A final story related to our visits in town had to do with the best bargain for the money that my older sister Kathy and I ever received: our first pairs of eyeglasses. What made it an even better bargain was that my parents paid.

A measurable quality of life change occurred for Kathy and me at 44 Bromfield Street in Boston, the location of our first optometrist. Kathy and I were generally A students in elementary school. However, our marks gradually started to decline because we couldn't see the teachers' writing on the chalkboard, maps, or even faces at a distance. We were visually impaired and didn't know it. My mother was advised to take us for vision testing. Thus, after school one day we went downtown to Gaeden and Kollitz Opticians on 44 Bromfield Street.

We sat for our eye exams and promptly both failed. We left the building a couple of hours later, Kathy fitted with salmon-colored glasses and I with the blue-framed ones I'd chosen. I am still in possession of that first pair of glasses, and pay homage to the eye doctors who were, at least in part, responsible for the improvement in our school performance. Mostly Kathy and I appreciated being able to see our favorite television shows more distinctly.

The odd memory that we both have is that the new glasses gave us distorted depth perception as we wore them for the first time. As we walked down Bromfield Street toward the subway home, we were forced to hold our mother's hands for our safety. As we were ten and eleven, we were humiliated to be seen this way. However, because of the depth distortion from our new corrective lenses, we saw hills on the sidewalks where there weren't any. We both walked like clowns, lifting our legs high and carefully placing each foot as if we were on stilts.

The glasses were prized possessions; they enhanced our ability to see and enjoy the world. They even made food choices better because now we could actually read the menus and select from a panoply of options. Gone were the days where we just chose what was written on the menu in the largest writing. I really got sick of "EARLY BIRD SPECIALS" as a young child.

Although I was a child when I got my first pair of glasses, I still treasure my improved vision. Decades later, I measure my success by how many pairs of eyeglasses I own. For all of the years that I could only afford one pair at a time, it was problematic when I needed them and couldn't remember where I left them last. Glasses hidden in the couch cushions meant that I could lose a whole day of work or school unless I found them. One night my spectacle-wearing husband and I both carelessly left our glasses in the living room. Our golden retriever puppy ate both, leaving behind chewed bits of frame and broken glass. We had to wait until we could convince a willing licensed driver to bring us both to the optometrist for replacements as soon as possible.

But now I own not one, or even two, but three pairs of glasses. This woman is a success! And all because of 44 Bromfield Street.

27

Down Victory Road

On my frequent visits to Dorchester for this book, I travel all the main streets and back alleys, trying to jog childhood memories. As I drive down Victory Road, I wonder why it feels so comfortable to sit in my car at the playground remembering days gone by. There are no standout stories about the playground—just happy days.

The playground was authorized to be constructed in 1958. It was designated as the Representative Phillip McMorrow Memorial Playground in memory of the former member of the general court from the fifteenth district. A Dorchester native and graduate of Boston Latin School, McMorrow was elected to the legislature in 1936 and later was the chief assessor for the city of Boston. I drove by the playground in early 2020 and was gratified to see that the plaque in McMorrow's name still stands.

When I lived in Dorchester, I often played at the Victory Road playground with my siblings and friends. The playground contained the standard equipment: swing set, metal slide, seesaw, monkey bars, and often a chalk-drawn hopscotch sketch on the ground for playing the rock-tossing and jumping game. Hopscotch was considered a girls' game, If I was just with females, I'd play that or do crafts with on-site youth counselors who worked at the playground.

In the absence of supervision, I was the ringleader of the daredevil merry-go-round crew. Typically my crew included Patrick

Donnelly and other boys if we were roughhousing. As the designated runner, I'd hang onto a metal bar while racing in ever faster circles until my mostly willing riders nearly spun into orbit—not the store, but outer space. (Orbit's, the department store, was further down the street.)

Our adventures at the playground were rather routine for the day. But the equipment, by later standards, was dangerous. There were no nets to catch children who fell from heights while climbing. The surfaces where we played were hard and unforgiving—sometimes concrete, sometimes asphalt, but often just bare ground where the grass had eroded from so much activity. However, the frequent presence of supervising adults or older siblings, and the absence of lawsuits for "normal" playground injuries, allowed 1950s safety standards to stick around for decades.

Of course we loved it. Although we often suffered from skin scalded by sun-heated metal slides, sharp edges which sometimes introduced tetanus after cutting open our skin, and head bumps from being pushed, pulled, or simply falling from the playground equipment, never did we have to cope with the insult of a sign that read, "No Running in Playground!"

As I continued down Victory Road, I would very often stop at the Dorchester Pottery factory. At the time it was probably a bit unusual for a young girl to frequent the factory. But I possessed a never-ending fascination with the Pottery Works and its products. As I write this in 2020, I have behind me a large curio cabinet chock full of Dorchester Pottery. At times, people have mistakenly corrected me and said, "You mean Dedham Pottery." I get very obviously rankled and admonish them by saying, "No, I said Dorchester Pottery and I meant Dorchester Pottery!" Suffice it to say, there is also a Dedham Pottery product line, and the reader is most welcome to look it up on the Internet.

Dorchester Pottery Works was established in 1895 on Preston Street (now Victory Road) in Dorchester. Dorchester Pottery Works produced hand-decorated home stoneware such as bean pots, casseroles, jugs, and mixing bowls in distinctive New England motifs, although the company originally had been founded by George Henderson to produce goods for commercial use. The stoneware required firing at 3000 degrees, much higher than earthenware, which only needed 1500 degrees. Thus, Dorchester

Pottery had a distinctive "beehive" kiln, fascinating to me as a child, in which their potters' handmade clay pieces were fired. In 1928, the original owner's son Charles Henderson, and his wife Ethel Hill Henderson, added decorative tableware. When the pottery business suffered during the Great Depression, Ethel began painting on the stoneware. Her distinctive designs included blueberries, pinecones, pussy willows, the sacred cod, and spouting whales. She revolutionized the business, breathing new life into Dorchester Pottery. After that, all their pieces were individually signed with the initials of the decorator. Those of us particularly familiar with their pottery recognize the initials painted onto each piece and the name of the artist who painted the pottery.

The last firing of the huge, custom-built beehive kiln took place in 1965. It was replaced by a small gas-fired one that lacked the beehive's charm. Business began to decline. The showroom was open only one day a week, and collectors lined up outside for the opportunity to purchase the increasingly rare pieces. I felt the loss of the showroom deeply as a child. Since I had been old enough to walk and do errands for my mother, if they took me to Victory Road, I visited the pottery shop. Once inside, I would study each piece, getting particular enjoyment from the bins of broken pottery pieces on the floor. I'd stand by each bin, running my fingers through the smooth edges of the broken pottery pieces, loving the feel and imagining their history. Decades later I became a serious collector. Their prices, even when the pieces achieved antique status, have never been prohibitive, although they would have cost me a lot less if I had spent my limited earnings on them back in 1965. To me, however, Dorchester Pottery is priceless, as are so many things, people, and places that remind me of my childhood home and life in the city. Arson gutted the pottery works and showroom in 1979, although the kiln room and the kiln itself remained intact. Both have been used for community exhibitions.

Typically, my next destination down Victory Road was Orbit's Department Store. Although I often went there with my family, on my solo trips I was most often doing an early morning errand for my mother. As my mother was always shy, and I never have been so, she would send me alone to Orbit's if she had an item to be returned.

But Orbit's was more often a family destination. The visits varied greatly in their outcomes. A happy trip for me was one during which I was allowed to purchase a kitten for sale for nine cents in a crate on display at the front of the store. I guess the product placement was such that shoppers might be reminded on the way out of the store that they had forgotten to buy a small, live animal. How convenient!

During the Easter season, baby chicks were sold from the same spot by the exit door, only the display case was an incubator, warmly heated and lit for maximum visual pleasure and olfactory offense. We begged my mother every spring to allow us to buy chicks when we were shopping at Orbit's for our Easter outfits. Her answer was a succinct, "No. They stink."

Orbit's Department store was a frequent destination for our family and plays a significant role in a variety of my childhood experiences. Orbit's was tied to Malibu Beach day trips with my sister Kathy. Kathy's penchant for persistent lateness got us both in trouble. We had absolute rules about getting home for supper so that we could all be sitting at the table together for my father's sacrosanct arrival time of 4:15 p.m. We have both always been shoppers, but Kathy has also always been a dawdler. I would get home in time just to keep a semblance of peace at the supper table. Kathy, if given the opportunity, would shop when the opportunity presented itself, no matter the consequences.

Once, when Kathy and I had gone to the beach together, we got a late start leaving, likely because Kathy had spotted an attractive male classmate from Saint Ambrose lounging shirtless on the beach. I couldn't convince her to leave on time. We finally got to the bridge in time for it to open unexpectedly to allow a boat with a tall mast to pass through. That delayed us a further ten minutes. By then I was frantic, trying to race home on sunburned feet. Kathy kept insisting that we had plenty of time to get home. As I ran, trying to drag her along with me, she spotted Orbit's and said that she needed to go in there immediately since she wanted to buy a pair of thong sandals which the store sold for pennies a pair. I insisted, "Kathy, we are going to get killed when we get home if we are any later than we already are!" She headed into Orbit's. I frantically followed her. She got her thongs and I dragged her bodily out of the store before she could shop anymore.

We arrived home late, and we were in big trouble. We might have been grounded, if that was a punishment option in our home, but the last thing my parents would ever do was to keep any of the kids *in* the house if there was any chance that we could be outside instead of underfoot! We got lectured, and lectured, and lectured by my father. As my own kids often did when I lectured them as punishment, we wished my father would just hit us and get it over with. Later in our bedroom, Kathy modeled the thongs for me, looking for my admiration. I threw them out the window after she fell asleep.

28

An Entrepreneurial Spirit

As a kid, I did anything I could to earn a bit of spending money. I loved to spend then, and I still do. At the time, I wanted enough to be able to buy a dill pickle, a new comic book, or a bag of potato chips at will.

I also had an entrepreneurial spirit as a child that came out in a desire to *get*. I got whatever I could that was free or discounted. Liggett's Rexall at the corner of Adams Street and Dorchester Avenue in Fields Corner once posted a sign advertising, "Buy one item, get the second for 1 cent." At ten years old, I was bold enough to walk in and ask the manager if I could just buy the second item for a penny without buying the first item at full price. He was too flabbergasted to answer, and finally sputtered that that was not how the promotion worked. I responded, "It was worth asking."

I earned money by babysitting nearly every day. I wove potholders and sold them in the neighborhood for 25 cents each or five for a dollar. I saved box tops from empty Rice Krispies cereal packages and redeemed them two at a time by mail for two shiny quarters. I did odd jobs and errands for neighbors for spare cash.

At one point my friend Joan and I packed eggs for Mr. Rooney down the street. He bought eggs in bulk and paid us fifty cents a night (two hours) to pack the eggs into cartons. We loved doing it because we could chat the whole time we worked. During one of our poorly thought-out discussions, we decided that we were not fairly compensated for our work, and we asked for a raise. We both got fired instead. That reduced my spending money noticeably.

But there was an answer. On the Dorchester Avenue end of Shepton Street was a thrift shop that not only sold used clothes and household goods but purchased them. I didn't own any household goods, but I did wear clothes. It occurred to me that I wore uniforms most of the time, and that I didn't really need that many clothes. For a period of time, I would go to the thrift shop and bring in my own clothes to offer to the owner for her perusal and possible purchase. She would often buy an item or two from me and I would walk out happily with anything from a dime to two dollars in my pocket. My limited wardrobe was dwindling as fast as I could read the new comics from Paul's Market on Florida Street.

I was down to one pair of shoes, and since there were a bunch of kids in my family, monitoring my clothing supply was not on my mother's priority list. The shopkeeper had told me that she would buy the shoes I was wearing, but I realized that I had to replace them with something else. The answer was at hand. Right there in the thrift shop was a pair of white vinyl sling backs for 20 cents. They looked like shoes to me. I sold the hard-soled shoes I was wearing to the proprietor for a dollar and put on what taunting kids later informed me were bedroom slippers. I donned them inside the store, questioning my decision, but it was too late. I already had plans for those 80 cents.

After a day or two, I was very embarrassed about the harassment I was getting from other kids about my poor footwear purchase. My mother finally noticed that I was wearing something odd on my feet, and she was afraid that the neighbors and the nuns would notice too. She asked me where my shoes were, and I shrugged. Nothing sends a mother to a kid's room faster than getting a shrug for an answer about why your clothes have been disappearing.

My mother was aghast when she saw what little clothing I had left, and I had already sold back the comic books for the two cents each that Paul would pay, so I had nothing to show for my wheeling and dealing. My mother asked my father to bring just her and me to Orbit's Department Store immediately after supper. Although she only said that I was outgrowing most of my clothes, he interpreted that as that I was getting too fat to fit into what I already had. I let him make that assumption rather than own up to what I had been doing.

I took the solitary ride with them to Orbit's. I should have been happy; I never got to go anywhere alone with my parents. But they were both mad. The nuns said that people didn't get mad, only dogs were mad. I guess my parents were dogs for the evening because they were really mad!

We got to Morrissey Boulevard and my mother handed me money and let me out of the car alone. She knew I knew how to shop for a bargain. I was her daughter, wasn't I? I immediately headed for the girls' sale rack. It was spring and I would need summer clothes since those were the first things I had sold the previous fall.

I casually grabbed an orange shirt and short set for five dollars. I hate the color orange, even more so now than I did then. But I was going to enjoy picking out an assortment of clothes, peruse them efficiently, and then choose what I could get for the $20 bill my mother had handed me. Suddenly I felt my mother's hand grasping my arm and warning, "Hurry up! Dad is really mad that I gave you 20 dollars. He said, "No wonder Judy was smiling going into the store! What kid gets 20 dollars to buy a new set of clothes?" Meaning that was a princely sum. Stunned at what I felt was a betrayal, I stood momentarily silent. My mother grabbed the orange outfit and the $20 bill and pulled me toward the cash register. I couldn't even think straight, but I knew that I had mistakenly chosen what might be my forever outfit. And it was orange! I never said a word about needing shoes too. I climbed into the back seat, eyes brimming with tears, as they drove home seething: my father at my mother, and my mother at me.

I was saved by a bag of hand-me-down clothes from my cousin Diane. We received these splendid outfits that were hardly worn after Aunt Connie went on another of her well-known spending sprees. This time, in addition to all the finery, there was a pair of everyday shoes. Real shoes. Barely worn. I was so thankful that I said a prayer to God and to Aunt Connie for her generosity with Diane's outdated or simply unwanted clothing.

One might think that I had learned a valuable lesson, but not quite. I took the white plastic sling-back slippers to the thrift store on Shepton Street the following morning and offered to sell them back to the owner for ten cents. She refused. I never went back there again. And now I am stuck with a possession obsession. I can't seem to have enough clothes or shoes at one time. Fortunately, the bargain-hunter in me thrives.

29

❦

Linda Mae's and the Chocolate Pudding Tarts

O f all of my favorite food places in Dorchester—well, there are simply too many to list, so I will focus on the bakery at the corner of Morrissey Boulevard and Victory Road, Linda Mae's. The beloved bakery and restaurant closed their doors in October of 1995 after a quarter of a century in business.

Linda Mae's was wildly popular in Dorchester with both residents and OFD (Originally from Dorchester) customers who had moved out of the city, out of state, or even out of the country, and religiously returned to Linda Mae's when circumstances or desire brought them back to Dorchester. For over 25 years, Linda Mae's served hearty breakfasts that were high in fat, cholesterol, and taste but low in price. As health consciousness changed, Linda Mae's adapted their menu to include more nutritionally sound offerings, while still keeping the most scrumptious foods for those who wanted them, despite the calories, fat, or sodium content.

Linda Mae's was known more as the first modern breakfast restaurant in Dorchester, in contrast to its early reputation as a bakery with a delicious array of offerings. But it was the bakery products I remember most. In the 1960s, people came to Linda Mae's in droves for sweets. The fabled restaurant and bakery was nearly always full of hungry customers.

One day, my Aunt Pat took Kathy and me to Linda Mae's where we could each pick out our own pastry. We wouldn't even have to share. It was a rare and welcome opportunity, however, my parents had strict rules about the time that we ate supper: 4:15 p.m. every workday, as soon as my father got in from work.

Aunt Pat had taken us to Malibu Beach that day to boot, and it was after 3:30 when we left the beach. Aunt Pat said that we would have to eat our pastry as we walked home. I was somewhat uncoordinated. I could not rub my belly in a circular motion while I patted my head—but nothing could make me lose my grip on a Linda Mae's pastry while I walked fast.

I chose the most desirable dessert that I laid my eyes on, an individual chocolate pudding tart covered in a mound of fresh whipped cream. I was in my glory. Aunt Pat paid and reminded us to keep walking as we ate. Suddenly we smelled smoke and looked up ahead of us where we saw flames flickering upwards from the Victory Road Railroad Bridge. Our first option was to wait for the fire department to put out the fire and risk being late for supper. The second choice was to dump the dessert and run, passing under the bridge before the fire department arrived and put up barriers. That might get us home on time, but we had no intention of discarding our desserts.

Along with my mother, Aunt Pat was one of the most obedient people I have ever met in my life. The WWJD bracelets popular when I was a youngish mother stood for "What would Jesus do?" My mother lived by that. As did my Aunt Pat. Both of them even went to Mass at Arch Street Chapel when it wasn't necessarily a Sunday or Holy Day of Obligation.

To our shock this time, our Aunt yelled, "Hang on to your desserts and run!" We didn't waste the moment that it would take to look shocked at her welcome flouting of safety rules. I did her one better. Because the intense heat so close by was starting to melt my whipped cream, threatening to send it sliding off the chocolate pudding tart, I ran as fast as I could while scarfing down the treat. We made it under the bridge safely and got home in time for supper.

The most memorable part of that day will always be my saintly Aunt Pat yelling "Run!" All for the sake of a Linda Mae's pastry and avoidance of a punishment for being late for supper.

One of my fondest memories with Aunt Pat was accompanying her to Codman Square to do the grocery shopping one day near noon. She spontaneously said, "Let's go to Heller's Deli." Aunt Pat suggested that we both have hot pastrami sandwiches on bulky rolls with mustard, a half-sour pickle, potato chips on the side, and a glass of ice-cold Coke. I thought I had died and gone to Heaven, it was all so delicious. Aunt Pat had unknowingly introduced me to what turned out to be a life-long love: hot pastrami on bulky rolls or Jewish rye, depending on the deli. In my adulthood, my husband and I are still stuck on hot pastrami sandwiches, which recall that bygone, much enjoyed lunch with Aunt Pat. But by now Heller's Deli is a distant memory. However, the memory keeps calling us for pastrami sandwiches. Our two favorite places for hot pastrami are Katz Deli in New York City, site of the famous scene from *When Harry Met Sally* with Billy Crystal and Meg Ryan, and Rein's Deli in Connecticut. I lick my lips as I write this and make silent plans to suggest to my husband that we take a trip to New York City via Amtrak from Boston this weekend to go to Katz's. The scene we will recreate will not be Meg Ryan's sensuous display of an amorous event but my own luscious recall of that first hot pastrami sandwich with dear Aunt Pat.

30

Grandpa Tom and Grandma Sadie Currivan

My mother's parents were a quiet and genteel couple. They were nearly ideal grandparents: soft-spoken, generous, and caring. In my lifetime I witnessed only one very minor altercation between them: My gentle grandmother once snapped at my grandfather for having given me a small gift. I was at their modest home and he dearly wanted to give me a little present. He looked around and spotted what appeared to me to be a miniature cast iron frying pan. I was a child who played with dolls until I was 13, and any small household items became accessories for my "children."

Grandpa took the item, rinsed it out carefully, and handed it to me. Grandma inexplicably got angry at him. I looked up in shock as she said, "Don't give that away! I wanted that!" I had never seen my grandmother act like this before. As I looked closely at the item in my hands, I noticed that it had a pair of indentations on opposite sides of the little frying pan. I figured out that it must actually be an ash tray. I didn't know why Grandma wanted to keep it as I had never seen either of them smoke. However, cigarette smoking was a very common habit in the early 1960s. Grandma was a gracious hostess and likely wanted to keep it available for guests. She said the same about the bottle of vodka in her hand when my cousin ran into her in a package store many years later. By then we were in our twenties and thought it was funny that our old grandmother was hiding her alcohol purchase from her grandson instead of the other way around. Suffice it to say, Grandpa convinced Grandma to let me keep the little frying pan-ashtray. But I never played with it because I always associated it with the discomfort I experienced from this soft-spoken couple having the rare argument in front of me.

My family was secretive for my entire life. That applied to nearly all of the adults on both sides of the family. There is so much that I am still learning about family history, and so much more that I will likely never know, despite intensive social and archival research on my part. Much of what I know came from my persistent habit of eavesdropping as a child. But I also asked questions—probably rather intrusive, but I simply wanted to know.

I asked Grandma Sadie numerous times about when she met Grandpa and when they got married. She evaded much of the issue but once inadvertently admitted to me that she had never wanted to get married. In fact, she was "old" for her time when she was finally convinced by her parents that marriage and bearing children was her duty. I have no knowledge of how she met Grandpa and agreed to marry him, but she made a wonderful, if reluctant, choice. They had five children together, three sons and two daughters, the youngest being my mother, Jean.

Grandpa Thomas Currivan was a humble man, and it was only research for this book that gave me proper knowledge of the admirable life he had led as a war hero and celebrated Boston Police officer.

A *Boston Globe* article from 1932 provided me with the information that Officer Thomas Edward Currivan of 33 West Tremlett Street, Dorchester, a member of the Boston Police Department since 1932, was presented by the U.S. Secretary of War with a Purple Heart Medal for Military Merit in the World War. Grandpa served with the American Expeditionary Forces (AEF). In September 1918, he had received a regimental citation for the taking of two German machine guns in the frontlines. A month later, while a private in Machine Gun Company 311th Infantry, he had been wounded in action.

Almost immediately following his discharge from the military, he was recruited to join the Boston Police Force, which was in the beginning stages of the Boston Police Strike of 1919. I interviewed the archivist of the Boston Police Department about this strike, as those who joined the force when the strike was taking place were considered "scabs," and the label stuck for decades. The archivist explained to me that it was unlikely that my dear grandfather joined as a strikebreaker, but that in the time of desperation for police coverage on the streets of Boston, men were actively recruited from the military, and hired with little preamble, if they were about to be discharged, and of high military rank. This was reassuring to me, as I knew my mother and her siblings often felt their heroic father had been stigmatized for having joined the BPD in 1919.

Grandpa Tom died on July 5, 1961, one month after the death of my paternal grandfather, Officer Thomas M. Kirwan of the Boston Police Mounted Patrol. Grandpa had been found by his wife, my grandmother Sadie Currivan, on the floor of their kitchen at 4 a.m. She called an ambulance and he was pronounced dead at 5 a.m. Grandpa Tom had been last seen by Grandma Sadie at 10 o'clock the night before, sitting in the kitchen, watching television, enjoying his nightly glass of whiskey.

Grandpa Currivan spent most of his 27-year career with the Boston Police in the Harbor Patrol. In the years between 1932 and his death announcement in 1961, more than forty articles about him appeared in the *Globe*. However, rarely did his daughter Jean, my mother, tell us anything at all about his activities. The one thing she ever mentioned was that he had been the officer to take the acclaimed child actress Shirley Temple for a ride on the Boston Harbor Patrol Police boat. Persistent research and a bit of serendipity led me to the details in a *Globe* story dated 1938: "Unable to forget the kindness and courtesy shown her by Boston's Finest on her recent visit to Boston, Shirley Temple, movie land's winsome child star, yesterday by mail conferred upon six officers of the [H]arbor [P]olice her own private Victorian Cross—the Shirley Temple junior police badge" and an autographed portrait "of her million-dollar smile."

But I found out that Lieutenant Thomas E. Currivan was noted in many of the articles as one of the "most skilled navigators in the area." He had a record of numerous Boston Harbor and sea rescues, many of which were written up in the *Boston Globe* and also in the *Boston Post*. In June of 1937, two young couples sailing together overturned their sloop *Idler* into the water of Hingham

Bay. Hampered by their clothing, the four had been struggling in the water for more than a quarter of an hour, clinging to the overturned boat and close to exhaustion, when the crew of the new Boston Police speedboat *Argus* rescued them. The *Argus* was on a trial run under the charge of Grandpa Tom and John J. Smith of the Harbor Police, who had been passing Sheep Island when they sighted the overturned sloop. Currivan and Smith pulled the four aboard the *Argus* and delivered them to the Point Allerton Coast Guard Station where they were provided with warm clothing and sustenance. The four victims said that when the police boat reached them, they had almost given up hope of rescue. None suffered serious ill effects in the incident.

Two years later in April, at South Boston's L Street pier, Sergeant Thomas Currivan and his Harbor Police associates on the *Michael H. Crowley* saved three workmen from being blown out to sea on a raft. Police headquarters had been notified by three different witnesses that the men were in a perilous position on a float, with nothing to aid them but long poles. Thomas Currivan at once headed the *Crowley* for the pier and took the men to nearby land. The men had thought that the wind would blow them not to sea, but in the opposite direction when they started out.

We were fortunate to have our grandmother Sadie Currivan in our lives for over two decades following Grandpa's death. Grandma was an independent woman who stayed involved with her family but lived alone for most of her remaining years. She loved shopping, primarily at her favorite thrift stores and discount shops. Her passions were her cat Baby, for whose favorite chicken livers she went to the butcher shop daily. If Grandma was short on money, she would go without eating herself, in order to buy Baby's chicken livers.

Behind this quiet exterior, she, like my mother, was reserved, but enjoyed having family around her. When we were pre-teens, Jeanie and I would sometimes take the bus from Ashmont to Wollaston, a section of Quincy where Grandma lived. Frequently, we'd stay overnight two or three days. The majority of the time, Grandma was teaching us to play card games. Like my other Grandmother, Ma Kirwan, Grandma saw this as serious business. Almost always kind, she once chastised me abruptly for my silliness during our hours of games. "You will never win this game! You don't have a poker face!" she said through clenched teeth. She was absolutely right. Nearly all of my emotions are fully discernible in my facial responses. And yet she still turned Jeanie and me into card sharks.

Our favorite game, which we continued playing at home for months, was gin rummy. We'd play in Jeanie's attic bedroom through the night, and if my mother happened to get up after midnight, she'd hear the rapid shuffling of cards and climb the stairs to send us to bed. Most often, she'd find us sitting nearly unmoving under the ceiling light, slapping cards down onto the floor, and picking up more cards as rapidly as we discarded the others. A game of gin rummy often extended to 500 rummy, and then to 1000 rummy, as we couldn't stop playing feverishly once we'd embarked on another game. My mother would take the cards from our hands and hide them, but the next day, one of us would run to the Five and Ten to purchase another deck of Hoyle playing cards.

Another way my mother and her mother were exactly the same was their intense sense of personal privacy. If they felt strongly that a matter was no one else's business, nothing could pry information from their tight lips. An extreme and painful example of this desire for privacy arose when I was in my early 20s. I knew a lot about nearly all of my aunts, uncles, and cousins. I knew that my mother had three brothers and one sister. We saw one of my mother's brothers and her sister very often. Accounting in my head one day, I asked my mother, "Why don't we ever see two of your brothers?" Nonchalantly, she answered, "I was never close to my oldest brother and the other one is dead."

In shock, I repeated, "Dead? Your brother is dead? When did he die, and why don't we know that?" She stayed placid as she answered, "It doesn't matter. You kids really didn't have any relationship with him." I persisted, "Mum, *when* did he die?" Again, she simply answered, "When you were 15." Finally, I asked in frustration, "How is it that your brother died and none of us kids knew about it?" Without expression she responded, "It is not your concern." She shut down the conversation. I closed my mouth but not my brain. I couldn't stop thinking about the fact that my mother had lost a sibling and we never even saw any sign that anything was amiss—no unexplained tears, no mood changes, just nothing.

I squeezed my brain for any dim memories of that time period in 1969. None came. As tenacious as I am, I had to know before I could let it go permanently. Based on my mother's absolute, stony-faced refusal to give up any other information willingly, I let it go . . . for the time being. Years later, a relative innocuously mentioned to me something about the time my mother's brother committed suicide. Based on my visible reaction, the relative tried to backpedal. I simply said, "I will never say anything to my mother about this, but will you just confirm to me what you just said?" I got the answer that I had never expected, and I never revealed to my mother that I knew. My reaction was only how tragic the whole situation was: My mother and her family had lost a member and resolved to never divulge the information; my uncle had suffered such internal pain for whatever reasons that he had taken his own life; he was never mentioned again by his siblings or mother; my grandmother had lost a son as a widow by that time, without her husband to console her; the depression and anxiety that haunted many members of both sides of our family had resulted in at least one self-inflicted death.

I think about my mother's brother often, even though I never knew him. I never spoke of him to my mother again, but I did take her often to visit my grandmother, who suffered from Alzheimer's and lived out her life in a nursing home. The nurses in the facility told me that in her confusion, my grandmother would often call out for her lost son. He was gone but never forgotten.

31

❧

5 Hopestill Street

The indomitable Edith Kirwan, my father's mother, was known as "Ma" to nearly everyone who met her. Those who either feared her or didn't know her well called her "Mrs. Kirwan." The rest of Dorchester just called her "Ma Kirwan."

As a grandmother, Ma Kirwan is fairly difficult to describe. She should have been a pro at the role by the time I was born. She gave birth to 11 children, one of whom died at birth. The 10 surviving children were born over a 20-year period, the first child arriving in 1914, the last in 1934. However, a couple of factors likely made a difference in both her mothering ability and her grandmothering style. First, Ma was an only child, and never had to deal with siblings of her own, much less the ever-fluctuating number of children underfoot in their substantial home in Dorchester. At last count, Ma and Pa had over 50 grandchildren, and that does not even include step-children or perhaps unacknowledged grandchildren.

There are a couple of significant reasons for her large number of progeny: She was married to a Boston-born Irishman, and the birth control pill was not legally available to married couples till 1965. It is likely fortunate that she *only* raised 10 children, although one newspaper account credits Ma with 12. Maybe she did have that many, but to my knowledge, there were "just" 10.

Relevant to the uncertainty over how many children belonged to Ma and Pa was the significant age difference between their oldest and youngest children. Children were being born to the oldest of Ma and Pa's kids before their own youngest were out of diapers. It must have been confusing how many belonged to them, and in what capacity.

And yet there is a much more significant reason Ma's knowledge and ability regarding mothering and the traditional role of wife at the time were different from most women her age. Ma was, above all else, a Dorchester Dame, and that is not meant in the regal way. Although Ma was English Protestant, she was born not in a castle across the pond but in New Jersey. Legend was that there was a castle bequeathed to her in England, but that decades went by before the Kirwan family learned Ma had inherited this impressive but rundown property. Unpaid back taxes on the possibly fictional castle would have rendered the inheritance moot in any case.

As such, Ma wore no crown. Also, no apron, no scrub gloves, and I never saw her wield a dust mop. Instead, her time was dedicated to three key areas of her life: church, Dorchester Dames, and the exquisite crocheting which took up a significant portion of her day when she was at home.

Ma converted to Catholicism when she married my grandfather, the Boston Irish cop. I heard she had been disowned by her parents for her match, but if she had truly been shunned, there must have been a reunion that was never discussed because Ma's mother's funeral was held in Ma's own home. Ma faithfully belonged to Saint Matthew's Parish for many years. She could be more than generous as a parishioner. After a spat with Pa before Mass one morning, Ma went to church in a snit. When the collection basket was passed around, she didn't fish in her pocketbook for coins or dollar bills—she threw in her gold wedding band. That was Ma.

She gave further evidence to her dedication to Catholicism by the presence of a rather ornate recreation of an altar that sat on her mantel. When she could no longer attend Mass in person, she watched morning Mass on television, which allowed her to combine her loves of praying and crocheting. One thing Ma didn't tolerate was children laughing or fooling around while Mass was on: She might miss a prayer or a double crochet on the hanky she was edging while worshipping.

Ma was best known for her absolute inability to cook. Pa would work his shift on mounted patrol with the Boston Police

Department and care for his oldest children until the two oldest daughters Edith and Julia were able to assume the care of each of the younger children as they came along and cook the meals for the family.

Ma's days and evenings were thus mainly occupied with the Dorchester Dames. We all grew up knowing that Ma played "cahds," but I never knew much about the Dorchester Dames until I researched what turned out to be quite a well-established organization. Unfortunately, despite an exhaustive search, I found no formal history of the Dorchester Dames. But archival research revealed hundreds of *Globe* articles, primarily in the social pages, referring to the Dorchester Dames in general, and to "Mrs. Edith Kirwan" or "Mrs. Thomas Kirwan" in particular.

Who were the Dorchester Dames? I had to find out. It turns out that Ma dedicated much of her adult life to this card-playing philanthropic organization until its demise in 1948. Originally an auxiliary of the Dorchester Club, the Dorchester Dames began in 1914. They held card parties at the Dorchester Clubhouse at 28 Talbot Avenue and in Franklin Hall on Melville Avenue, plus other venues throughout the city, as well as in members' homes. Their fundraising supported furlough homes (where soldiers could rest and recreate during short respites from fighting lines during the two wars), hospitalized former servicemen, Saint Phillip's Church, a young woman who was to enter the convent, an unnamed family in need.

Ma rose to prominence in the Dorchester Dames in 1938 when she became a frequent hostess of their card-party fundraisers in clubhouses and in her home at 5 Hopestill Street in Dorchester. Even after the Dames' demise, Ma received sporadic news coverage for her continuing contributions to charitable work in Dorchester and Boston. Interestingly, her later endeavors often involved children, although Ma had little tolerance for actual children. In fact, Ma's most significant engagement in the Dorchester Dames began when her youngest of ten was only 4 years old.

Again, Ma's inability to cook was legendary. Older cousins told me she had one (1) standard set of directions for cooking: 350 degrees Fahrenheit for 45 minutes, no matter what was to be served. Thus cooking—when not done by her older daughters and Pa—was left to guests, or any stranger who could wrangle a skillet and spatula and might be walking by the house. Oscar Wilde had foreknowledge of her when he wrote, "The British cook is a foolish woman, who should be turned, for her iniquities, into a pillar of that salt which she never knows how to use."

With so many people in the family, and her relatively small dining room, it was rare to have large groupings at Ma and Pa's for a holiday meal. Typically, we ate at our respective homes and came to Ma's for dessert. One Thanksgiving when I was about 12, my family was invited to dine with Ma, Aunt Pat, and Cousin Bobby. It was unusual for just one family to be chosen to have the main meal at 5 Hopestill Street, but hungry we came. Ma was hovering over the small stove when we arrived. Our assumption, since Pa was deceased by this time, was that Aunt Pat must have cooked dinner. But no, Ma was fussing around the oven as she directed my sisters and me to set the table. We gathered that my father, the oldest male at the table, would be given the stereotypically masculine role of carving the turkey.

After a period of time, we were called to dinner and the mashed potatoes, squash, and cranberry sauce were placed on the dining room table. Our mouths were watering for what was to come, but we didn't detect the delicious aroma of roasted turkey skin or hear the sizzling of hot grease as it slid off the bird into the pan, making drippings for the gravy. Ma told us all to sit, and she struggled to get the 25-pound turkey out of the oven by herself. In her intended projection of the role of kindly grandmother providing for her family with the traditional Thanksgiving centerpiece, she refused any and all assistance. We sat salivating, and Ma made her proud appearance bearing the highly anticipated roasted turkey.

Instead, there was a pale, flaccid mound on a serving platter, and it appeared to have blood pooling around it. We all silently gagged. Aunt Pat was the only one bold enough to address her mother, with whom Aunt Pat and her son Bobby lived. Aunt Pat cried out, "Jesus, Mary, and Joseph! *Ma!* How long did you cook that?" Ma, furious that her culinary skills were being questioned, answered (as we should have expected), "45 minutes at 350 degrees!" The cold, dead bird was rapidly removed from the dining room, and we feasted on mashed potatoes, squash, cranberry sauce, and rolls. Other aunts arrived carrying an array of traditional, fully cooked, desserts. It was a delightfully non-nu-tritious Thanksgiving feast, and yet it gave us full stomachs and a new tale to tell about Ma Kirwan of Dorchester.

Now, the irony is that this woman hosted large social lun-cheons and dinners for most of her life. She had impressive social presence. But if you wanted a good meal with Ma, it was best to invite her to *our* home where my own mother could have taught Julia Child a thing or two. Unlike her feisty mother-in-law, my mother was shy, quiet, and the apparent model 1950s housewife and mother.

Ma still managed to make the papers as a prominent Dorches-ter police wife, happy homemaker, loving mother of some indeter-minate large number of kids (it was never quite clear, even in the newspaper), and organizer of charitable events. As the December 13, 1946 *Boston Globe* headline put it: "Co-chairmen of Party for 200 children have 22 of their own." Here's the math:

> *Two mothers who have a total of 22 children of their own are co-chairmen of a Christmas party to be given by Boston Police Wives Association for 200 children Sunday afternoon at 2:00 at the Knights of Columbus Hall, Pea-body Square, Dorchester. Mrs. Edith Kirwan of 5 Hopes-till Street has provided Christmas entertainment for her own 12 children over a period of 33 years, while Mrs. Alice Davis of Eden Street has done the honors for her ten chil-dren. Candy, toys, and ice cream will be distributed by Santa Claus in the person of Officer James McKenna of 50 Edson Street, Dorchester. Mrs. Eileen Brooks, president of the association, will direct the party.*

32

⤜∾⤛

The Problem with Free Candy

Although she could not cook, Ma was not averse to grocery shopping, and even had a favorite butcher shop, Sam's. First National Stores (FINAST) in Codman Square was adequate for her household staples but nearly everything else was purchased from Kaspar's. Being the one or two of her dozens of grandchildren chosen to accompany Ma to the friendly neighborhood market on Norfolk Street was a favorite event. Mr. Kasparian was the owner and close friend to the woman who likely provided much of his livelihood with her huge brood. He was a gregarious man, and kind to Ma's young helpers. She'd send us throughout the store according to her list, while they gossiped. We'd hear lots of laughing, interspersed by low voices when we were not supposed to be privy to certain parts of their conversations.

The absolutely delightful part of the event, however, came as Ma paid her bill, and Kaspar sauntered over to the candy counter. Each time, he'd pick up a pack of Charms candy (like square Lifesavers with no hole in the middle), hold it in the direction of her shopping helper and ask, "Ma, is it ok if I give these Charms to your grandchild who was so good as to help you today?" We danced in excitement waiting to receive the candy, knowing that this was all pre-arranged, and that Ma would not deny us this delicious pleasure. We also knew that we were expected to share the package of candy with our siblings or cousins waiting back at 5 Hopestill Street.

The excitement of receiving the treasured gift was only exceeded by being the one to carefully unwrap the precious package and take out and eat just the first candy. That candy was the only one enjoyed in the solitude of the walk back to Ma's. Once inside, clamoring siblings and cousins would tear apart the rest of the package like a pack of jackals with a piece of meat. We never argued about who *had* to help Ma at Kaspar's. We argued over whose privilege it was to go to the friendly grocer with the generous spirit.

Kaspar's generosity, however, skewed my perceptions of another grocer, my friend Linda's father and the primary owner of Leonardi's Superette. Linda and I met at Saint Ambrose in first grade in September of 1960. Near my Parkman Street triple-decker but a world away was, to me, a magnificent mansion—Linda's family home.

I was intrigued by bubbly Linda, her huge house, and her married sister living with her husband in the house. If I stayed overnight, Linda would drag me upstairs the following morning to where her sister and husband were sleeping late, and Linda would bounce on the bed, the adored little sister teasing her sister and brother-in-law. I never knew another child who had a brother-in-law. Further, I never ever had seen any of my friends' family members in their beds. It was all overwhelming to me, although completely respectable. But it deviated from the norm.

Also different was that an unmonitored, one-pound box of chocolates was typically on the dining room table. That was another thing: Linda's house had a kitchen table *and* a dining room table. With nobody guarding the candy! Linda was permitted to open the box at will and have a piece of chocolate. She didn't have to ask anybody, and she was always generous in offering me a piece. I furtively accepted it and gulped it down before somebody came to yell at me. But that never happened at Linda's.

About two years into our friendship, the Leonardis opened a grocery store on Dorchester Avenue, just a short walk from their home. This incredibly hard-working family sold an array of groceries along with memorable deli sandwiches, and homemade breads and pastries every day of the year. Even on Christmas Day, Leonardi's was open, although they closed at 2 p.m. instead of 10 p.m. Leonardi's was legendary. It stayed in business for over two decades.

And yet Kaspar had spoiled me for life. His free Charms candies drove me to lie to my family about my first experience at Leonardi's.

Linda's family had bought the land for the store from the Boston School Committee in 1959. A two-room Dorchester High School built in 1850 occupied the plot, a boarded-up eyesore in the neighborhood. The Leonardi family tore down the old school, and initially built Leonardi's Superette there. In 1962, the day before the store officially opened, Linda invited me for a preview. I was ecstatic. I felt like a celebrity, and assumed that, just as Kaspar did, Mr. Leonardi would offer me free candy. It wouldn't even have to be Charms, as much as I loved the package of hard candies.

Linda proudly opened the front door of the store just for me that day. I hoped people would see me, Judy Kirwan, through the plate glass windows, and assume that I was someone special to be in Leonardi's before its premiere. Linda gave me the grand tour, and then we came to its end, approaching the front door.

Mr. Leonardi seemed a bit grumpy that day to me, an eight-year-old who could have no possible comprehension of the pressure he must have been under the day before his grand opening. What *I* noticed was that he didn't seem to be offering me any free candy. I looked at Linda as she sauntered around her family store and wondered why she wasn't just taking food off the shelves to consume freely. She got to do that with the candy on the dining room table, although I did notice that she never helped herself to more than one piece. But seriously, they owned the whole store. Surely, we could each have a free pack of candy. But no, we were done with the tour, and we left, and then she waved goodbye and went home to the family manse.

As I walked down Parkman Street, my juvenile self felt sullen. How could I ever admit to my family that I had had free rein in a brand-new grocery store and yet not been offered anything but a preview? What else could I do to save face? I had to lie. I remember describing to my envious siblings the grand store and all its delicious offerings. Of course, my siblings asked, "What did you get?" A few hands reached out for their compulsory share of whatever it was. I shrugged and said, "Oh, just some candy that we had to eat there." I don't know why I added that, but since we didn't know whether Italians had special on-site eating rules, no one questioned me about not having brought free candy home. My lesson from this was, "Blessed is she who expects nothing, for she will never be disappointed."

33

"We'll Take a Cup of Kindness Yet"

A Scots language poem written by Robert Burns in 1788, "Auld Lang Syne," is what comes to mind when I think of my Boston Irish paternal grandfather, Thomas Michael Kirwan, born in 1892. The title translates to "days gone by" and the cup of kindness is how I remember Pa.

Although I loved his wife, my Dorchester Dame grandmother Ma Kirwan, memories of her elicit altogether different sentiments than do memories of Pa. I wish I could say that I am more like Pa, but it's been said that I am exactly like my father, who was very much his mother's son.

To the outside world, Pa and Ma had ownership of their traditional gender spheres. Ma's was ostensibly home and hearth, and Pa's was the workplace. In fact, Pa was the kind, nurturing, loving man who toiled at his job as a Boston Police Officer, Mounted Division, in order to support his large family. But he never sought acclaim, awards, or climbing the law enforcement ladder. Pa met and married Edith Westcombe Kirwan and resided in East Boston at 309 East Eagle Street. As a young married man, Pa was a machinist. Later, he and Ma ran a small market while raising the first few children in their growing family. Pa also cooked, cleaned, and thoroughly engaged with all of the children, grandchildren, and neighborhood kids while Ma was occupied with her many social engagements.

Pa joined the Boston Police Department in November of 1926, older than most of the new recruits at 34, and already the father of five children. While Ma ruled the house with an iron fist, Pa was a kind and gentle man. When I think of him, I see his twinkling eyes, his broad smile, his ruddy skin, and hear his laughter. Ma was stern, strict, and far less affectionate than Pa. Pa embraced everyone, and favored his sweet and shy youngest daughter-in-law, my mother Jean. My reticent mother was vocal in her adoration of her father-in-law.

Pa was a hugger, a squeezer, a joker, and generous to his ever-growing family. He loved his job, but even as a professional law enforcement officer, his favorite task was escorting schoolkids across the street, giving a pat on the back to each and sharing a joke as they safely crossed. For many years of my childhood, a photograph of this scene greeted anyone who came into their dining room. Their sideboard was a long, flat-topped cabinet whose surface was home to all important mail and a few, very special, family pictures. The place of honor on the sideboard was the picture of Pa in his uniform, surrounded by children, as he stopped traffic and blew his whistle for the happy bunch on their way to school. The children surrounded Pa, beaming back at his smiling face, as he was always quick with a compliment or a joke for his charges.

A treasured photograph of Pa on my own dining room wall is of Pa and the entire Mounted Police force lined up, side-by-side on their horses in ceremonial formation. Although somber in the formal group portrait, Pa is immediately recognizable in the group because of his smiling eyes. I smile back at his picture each time I look at it. I believe that he smiles back.

One of Pa's favorite times of year was Christmas. He loved to give gifts to all of the kids. His standard gift was a red envelope. What was most special to us about these envelopes was that they held a surprise. It was not the fact that they held cash that made us hold our breaths as carefully as our outstretched hands. Pa loved to give out the envelopes, but he himself didn't seem to think about differential value of the gifts. To Pa, a gift was a gift. To his grandchildren, nieces, and nephews, the pleasure lay in opening the envelope. One might contain a $10-bill, another a single dollar, and another some other denomination, although it is doubtful any reached higher than $20. But his laughter was contagious. I don't recall anyone ever complaining if their envelope held a smaller amount than others. If Pa was laughing, we were all laughing.

Pa mastered cooking skills of necessity. Until the oldest of their kids could feed the younger ones, Pa prepared meals for the family. As Ma had birthed two females early in her line of descendants, it was as if she had contributed two surrogate mothers to the family; why cook? As a daughter of one of the surrogate mothers, much of my cousin Connie's early years were spent at 5 Hopestill Street. My father was 15 years younger than his sister, my cousin Connie's mother Julia. Yet he died from chronic heart disease just months before she died of congestive heart failure. When her family came to break the terrible news to her that her baby brother had predeceased her, she responded, "I've just lost my first child." To Julia, the younger siblings were her loving responsibility, even though she had a very large family of her own.

Food was always scarce, due both to the size of the traditionally very large families in Irish Dorchester, but also because of low wages. Cousin Connie told me that she would, as a child, often eat at the table side-by-side with Pa, enjoying his happy demeanor and savoring the small portions of food that were available for the ever-present crowd at the house. We didn't grow up eating dinner rolls, and we never knew anyone who did. Instead, accompanying supper was always a slice of white bread. If there was any to be had, margarine, or far less commonly, a pat of butter topped the bread. Connie would focus on her meager meal, and reach for her slice of bread, only to find it gone. She'd look at Pa, seated beside her, and he'd be happily chewing, and nod his head to acknowledge her gaze. Connie would wonder if she had scarfed down the bread so quickly that she had forgotten. Puzzled, she'd glance again at Pa, and he would benevolently smile, and continue chewing. This occurred with increasing frequency until Connie finally caught Pa in the act of sneaking her bread. He never admitted that he had taken her food, but after that, Connie never again put her bread down while she ate supper.

Pa, as was common at the time, occasionally used his status as a police officer for preferential treatment, not for himself, but for his grandchildren. He would often be detailed to the Boston Red Sox games. Cousins Paul and John Sullivan, both close to my age, would take public transportation to Fenway Park, where they would tell the ticket taker that their grandfather was doing a detail. The ticket taker would escort the boys to Pa's location, and Pa would kindly ask paid seat holders to give up their preferential seating in favor of more humble seating, explaining simply that he "needed" their seats for his grandsons. My cousin Paul said that no one ever turned down Pa's sweetly motivated request.

He would buy Paul and John cups of popcorn in conical tubes. After they ate the popcorn, a removable cap could be pulled off the popcorn container, allowing them to use it as a bullhorn. Following the game, Pa would drive both boys home in his car with the rotting floorboards. These afternoons remain unforgettable to my cousins.

Cousin Paul was also the unofficial lookout for Pa's dog Scotty who would sit patiently outside "Pa's Bah" (barroom) not far from the house. When it was time for Pa to come home for supper (cooked by almost anyone in the home except Ma), Ma would send Paul down searching for Scotty. Scotty was Pa's faithful canine companion, well known to the bar's patrons. As Pa and friends raised a glass or two, Scotty would scavenge for food. He'd go from one table to another begging for scraps. He was often rewarded for his polite begging. However, wartime rationing started affecting food supplies in the bar, and people had fewer scraps to give. Once, when Scotty had been turned down at a number of tables after begging, the disgruntled dog walked to the corner of the bar, lifted his leg, and urinated on the bar. He was "barred" from the tavern after that but would sit patiently for hours outside waiting for Pa to come out to go home. Thus, when Ma sent Paul looking for Pa, Paul only had to walk down the street far enough to see the front of the bar. If Scotty was outside, Pa was inside.

Pa, the quintessential Officer Friendly, with his smiling face and winning personality, was frequently ill during his career. By 1950, he was hospitalized often with what is described in his police records as "heart ailments." In 1952, he retired on disability through the "Heart Bill" at the rank of Patrolman, Division 16, his family having been his most illustrious "career."

After retirement, Pa was at home in declining health, but still very much a contributing member of the family. By the early 1960s, he spent most of his time confined to bed due to hypertensive heart disease and renal damage, but his personality was fully intact. The family would simply entertain him in his bedroom.

On May 1, 1961, Pa was in his bedroom when he suffered a heart attack. An ambulance was called to bring him to the hospital. From the stretcher, he called to Cousin Paul to run back to his bureau and grab Pa's statue of Our Lady of Fatima. Paul quickly grabbed it and handed it to Pa, who breathed his last breath with the statue held against his chest.

Should auld acquaintance be forgot? Never Pa Kirwan.

34

Tallulah

Every animal aficionado knows the joys and the sorrows of pet ownership. When I was four years old and living in Fields Corner, I had a blue parakeet named "Chippy." I woke up each morning to hear his early chirping as my mother removed the small blanket covering his cage. I was delighted to have my own little pet. On my last birthday, my mother had walked with me from our home on Faulkner Street to Woolworths on Dorchester Avenue and bought the bird for me. Chippy was a delightful pet, but we were unaware at the time that a local Five and Ten was not an appropriate place to purchase an animal. Profit, not proficient animal care, was the motive for selling live animals as pets.

Soon after I fell in love with Chippy he got sick. My mother and my older sister Kathy hurried to Woolworths to ask what might be a remedy for a sick bird. They were sold some product, unlikely at the recommendation of a veterinarian. Despite their best efforts to bring home the treatment that might save my parakeet, he was dead by the time they returned from the store just a few minutes away. My mother offered to replace my pet. I sadly said "No, thank you." Like most children, we had the same event occur repeatedly with the fishes and the turtles that we begged to own. Once again, longevity is a problem, especially when animals are obtained by mass sales from incompetent animal caregivers.

My parents allowed us to have Snoopy a couple of years later. He was a yellow cat who happily slept in the laundry basket, especially when we were among the first on the street to have a clothes dryer. There was nothing as pleasurable for Snoopy as climbing in among some toasty warm blankets for an afternoon nap. But being an outdoor cat, as virtually all pets were at the time, he succumbed to death after a couple of years of ownership. Again, the tears of small children (and their parents as well).

At some later point, my parents brought the four of us kids together in the kitchen: Kathy, Jeanie, little Lonnie, and me—and it wasn't even for a punishment! As my parents embraced, they asked us if we would like to have a new baby, or a puppy. We three girls shouted happily, *"A baby!"* My younger brother said just as loudly, *"A puppy!"* We got both, but the puppy came sooner than did infant Christine.

We delighted in Frisky and his adorable puppy habits. Frisky loved a good plateful of leftover spaghetti. But he would walk in circles around the plate successively chewing off neat mouthfuls of food until his full belly couldn't accommodate the mound of pasta and sauce he then left dead center on the plate. Frisky also resolved our conflict over an extra donut one morning. Four of us were nagging my mother to be allowed the last donut. A half-dozen had allowed for four kids and my mother to each have one. That last one was sitting on a plate, too irresistible for us not to fight over it. We all got closer and closer to just grabbing the remaining donut when Frisky suddenly leaped up, snatched it from the edge of the table, and gobbled it down. We all laughed so hard that we forgot to cry. We had all wanted that donut! Naturally sharing might have solved the problem, but Frisky saw it the way we kids had! He won and we laughed for weeks. Completely unrelated to his gobbling of the glazed treat, he succumbed to distemper. These situations happened to our pets over the course of a few years, but they were cumulative in their results. I lost heart for the ownership of pets, at least until we moved to West Roxbury for a year when I finished sixth grade.

One afternoon I accompanied my parents on errands around the semi-suburban West Roxbury and Roslindale neighborhoods of Boston. We now had a roomy single-family house, and a good-sized backyard. It was rare for me to be alone with my parents, but Kathy was old enough to babysit the other kids in the family.

As we drove along American Legion Highway, we came upon a truck at the side of the road with a sign that read, "Puppies $10."

I had not even thought about wanting a puppy, and suddenly, I couldn't have desired one more than I did at that moment. Half-holding my breath, I asked if we could stop and look at the puppies. I fully expected an adamant, *"no"* for an answer. To my surprise, my parents looked at each other, nodded and semi-reluctantly said "OK . . . but just to look," and I leaped out of the car. I dropped to my knees cuddling one puppy after the other until one female climbed into my lap and snuggled me. I was in love. "Mum and Dad," I begged, "could we *please* get this puppy? I would take care of it every day. I even have the money for it." Apparently, this was not really the spontaneous happening that I thought it was, because once again, they were willing to discuss it. "Puppies cost a lot to feed and for veterinary care," they argued. I answered, "I'll pay for it all! I babysit at least once a week for neighbors and relatives, and I earn money other ways!" Again, they feigned reluctance, but I saw that there was a possibility, and I all but sold my soul for the chance to take that puppy home as my own. It happened. She was mine!

Always one with a fondness for drama, I couldn't possibly name her Lady, or Missy, or Sandy. Instead, to the consternation of friends my own age, I named her "Tallulah" after the noted actress Tallulah Bankhead. The actress meant nothing to me, but I loved the unusual name. I built Tallulah a doghouse by myself in West Roxbury, although she never slept anywhere but at the foot of my bed. She and I became devoted to each other. At the appropriate time, my parents said it was time to have her spayed. I had saved for this and my mother drove us to the veterinarian in Dorchester to leave Tallulah for her neutering surgery.

In the same time period, for numerous reasons, my parents decided that we would move out of the city and to the suburbs. That meant that first we had to move back to our home on Edwin Street in Dorchester to ready the property for sale. To my despair, we moved out of Dorchester permanently once the house sold.

One September morning, I walked from Edwin Street to Ma's house in Codman Square to do Ma's errands. I made sure to lock the gate so as to keep Tallulah fenced in, particularly due to her recent surgery. She was still wearing bandages from the spaying, and I did not want to take a chance on straining her stitches by bringing her to Codman Square with me.

On arriving at 5 Hopestill Street, I visited Ma for a while, got the shopping list from her, and went up Aspinwall Road to First National Stores. While paying for the groceries at the front of the store, I heard the unmistakable screech of truck tires, a thud, and people yelling. I looked out to see Tallulah lying gravely injured on Dorchester Avenue. I was dazed with disbelief. I truly blocked out the possibility that it was my dog that had just gotten hit. I finished paying for the groceries, carried them across the street, and saw a large cardboard box on the street outside the Christian Science Reading Room. In a fog, I put down the groceries and went over and pulled the box away. As soon as I saw bandages, I couldn't deny to myself that it was my Tallulah. A woman came running out of the Reading Room, grabbed my shoulders to pull me away, and yelled, "Little Girl! Don't do that. That dog is dead!" I looked at the woman blankly and answered, "It's my dog." The woman tried to embrace me to comfort me, but I just pulled away in total disbelief.

I walked back to Ma's house, never saying a word about what had happened and watched as she reviewed my purchases against her list. Ma laughed and said, "I told you to get three pounds of oranges and you got three bags instead. They are three pounds per bag." I must have looked semi-hysterical although I wasn't showing any real outward emotion. She just reassured me, "It's okay. The oranges will get eaten." I woodenly said, "I have to go home now." I walked home forcing each step back to Aspinwall Road, to Washington Street, to Talbot Avenue, to Welles Avenue, to Dot Ave, to Shepton Street, to Denvir Street, and down to 53 Edwin. My mother was standing at the gate to the backyard when I got home. I still didn't cry. I asked her, still in a state of shock, "Where's Tallulah?" She answered, "Don't you know? Someone opened the gate shortly after you left, and she ran after you. Didn't she follow you?"

Apparently, my puppy had been devious enough to not let me see her as she followed me to Ma's. The realization slammed into me and tears poured down my cheeks. I went into the house and lay on my bed for a while as in our house, expressions of deep emotion were frowned upon. I cried quietly for a while by myself then got up, feeling shattered but once again showing little outward distress. I walked up Edwin Street to where my friends were playing. They immediately asked me, "Where's Tallulah?" as she was my constant companion. Well, she had been. Again, I simply answered, "She got killed today." They started to laugh as if I had told a sick joke, then saw my face and quieted immediately. I just looked at Cathy and Claire O'Malley and didn't say another word. Claire asked me gently, "Isn't it your birthday tomorrow?" It was. I didn't answer, but I felt that I would never again have another happy birthday in my life.

My grief was overwhelming, but I stifled it. It came out another way, however. I was unable to become emotionally attached to dogs for almost 18 years. My family had a series of small breeds over the years, and I was emotionally unable to care about any of them. I was still too fragile. At one point, my parents had two Shih Tzus, Suzie and Chu Chu. Suzie was whiny and snapped at the small children in our family. Chu Chu was sweet, but I still couldn't love any dog after Tallulah.

One afternoon I learned that Suzie was at the veterinarians after having been slightly injured when a car struck her. My heart opened again. I picked her up and held her when she returned home from the veterinarian's with minimal injury to her forehead. I felt such profound relief that she had survived being struck by a car. I cuddled her and was able to take the protective cage off my heart. I had never lost my ability to love cats or any other animal, but the shattering grief of seeing my own dog killed when I was a child had finally gone away. From that day, when Suzie got hit when I was in my 30s, my own home has housed an unending stream of cats and dogs. Currently, *only* three cats and three dogs are part of our household. They, along with my three daughters and their families, including six grandchildren, keep my heart full every day.

I still love you, Tallulah.

35

⌒⌒

Don't Call Dad at Work

We Kirwan kids were told never to call my father at Codman and Shurtleff in Savin Hill, where he worked as a surgical instrument maker; never to interrupt his workday for any reason whatsoever. As my parents were quite literal in their directives, I had no reason to question the decree. I was not known for unquestioning obedience to authority for its own sake, but there were serious consequences for misbehavior both at home and at Girls' Latin School. Thus, I pretty much toed the line. But that is no guarantee that things won't go awry.

A lifelong tendency toward clumsiness emerged during my adolescence. As a young kid, I was actually somewhat athletic, not compared to other kids who truly possessed physical skills, but relative to my non-sporty family. I rode my bike all over Dorchester, becoming so at ease with my control of the bike that I could get up to a speed enough to balance the bike, swing my rump onto the crossbar, pedal a bit from the side to keep the momentum of the bike going, and then resume the normal bike-riding position. As often as I did this crazy maneuver, I never fell, and never got hurt.

My friends and I vaulted hydrants without incident, shimmied up street poles, and thought nothing of lying prone on the street to fish down sewers for coins using coat hangers with a wad of chewed Double Bubble gum on the end. It was a simple, totally unforeseen, event that sent me to Carney Hospital in the middle of a gym class at Girls' Latin.

I could still lob a well-aimed volleyball, and also beat the rest of my class in our dance performances. So, it was with little concern that I sent a ball flying over the volleyball net but missed my footing and came down on my right wrist. I jumped back up, not feeling any pain, but apparently the greenish discoloration of my skin and the rolling of my eyes in my head indicated to the gym teacher that all was not well with me. She grabbed me and steered me to the nurse's office while I protested loudly, "Let me go back to class, I'm fine!" She ignored me and told the nurse that I was injured. My near faint when the gym teacher gently manipulated my wrist and forearm convinced them that I had to go to the hospital. I was about to get my coat for the less than one-and-a-half-mile walk to Carney. They laughed and said, "Judith, sit down and we'll call your father."

"Call my father?" I practically screeched, "No one is allowed to call my father at work!" They said they would call my mother to get me and take me to the hospital, but I reminded them that my father drove the one family car to work. I promised them that if they just let me finish out the school day, I would ask my father to take me to the doctor's after he had supper with us at 4:15 promptly. I figured that I could get to the hospital by 5:30 p.m. and still get home in time for homework. But these thoughts were all just that. By the time I had formulated this plan, the nurse had my father on the phone within 15 minutes of the injury taking place. I was aghast! While I quivered in the nurse's office, still insisting that I was fine, my father came into the office, signed me out, and headed toward Carney Hospital on Dorchester Avenue. Too late, I remembered that I was wearing my blue gym bloomers and white blouse, white bobby socks, and sneakers. Girls were never seen outside of the house dressed in such unladylike attire unless it was mid-summer. I was mortified.

It got worse, of course. We signed into Carney Emergency Room and my father picked up a magazine, confident that we'd have a while to wait before I would be x-rayed. I furtively looked around the waiting room, in dread of finding that someone had seen me, dressed as I was. My discovery shamed me! Sitting across from me in the ER, eyes averted, was a boy my age in a gym uniform as well. He had apparently gotten injured in his class, and ended up there, in what I thought to be a twisted coincidence, at the same time as I did. I picked up a magazine and hid my face. It may have been upside down in front of me, however it was unlikely that the boy would have noticed as he seemed as humiliated as I was. He kept his eyes averted from my flushed face and, in my view, my skimpy outfit.

I was finally called in to see the ER physician. He took my mind off my shame, and pronounced that I did, in fact, have a broken wrist bone, the radius, and that I would need a cast for two weeks. Finally, something useful was about to come out of this. I wouldn't be able to do dishes that entire time. (That was only partly true; my mother excused me from plunging my hands into the deep kitchen sink for scrubbing dishes and pans, but she determined that I was well able to dry and put away the freshly scrubbed implements. Drat.)

I loved the doctor. He chatted away with me as he casted my broken wrist and asked where I went to school. When I answered that I went to Girls' Latin School, it was apparent that he was a Boys' Latin grad, as he immediately said to me, "*flunko, flunkere, faculty fixum!*" I managed my first laugh of the day and then sidled out the back door of the ER, where I caught a glimpse of gym boy whose arm was also encased in a cast.

The doctor didn't scare me, but I was still afraid of what I would have to hear from my father for having him summoned from work. However, nothing dreadful ever happened because my father had left Codman and Shurtleff during a manufacturing shift to bring me to the hospital. In fact, it was such a non-event in my family that when I arrived home from Carney Hospital at my usual school dismissal time that my mother told me to change my clothes and get ready for Confraternity of Christian Doctrine (CCD, my after-school religion classes). Wow, a broken limb and I couldn't even score one extra privilege in our strict household!

When I got to CCD, my teacher commented on the number of unexcused absences in that day's class. She was not happy; we were in our preparation program for Confirmation. Without seeing me, she pronounced relative to all the absences, "The only good reason for ever missing CCD is if you have a broken arm." I raised the cast, thinking that maybe she would let me go home. That didn't happen. She simply laughed and said, "Well, maybe that is not a good enough reason to miss." Although she did express surprise when she asked me when the fracture had happened, and I answered that it had occurred just a couple of hours prior to CCD.

Yes, my parents had a reputation, and it wasn't for leniency. The only good part about having really strict parents was that if we were ever tempted by our friends to engage in significantly deviant conduct, we could simply answer, "I'd love to do that with you, but you know my parents. They'd kill me!" My friends just nodded sympathetically and acknowledged that the next time they'd see me would be at my final services.

The important lesson that I learned from all of this was that we actually *could* call Dad at work. But the call was only justifiable for a fractured limb or worse!!

36

⚜

"Mrs. Kirwan, Call the Police!"

With my father once again away from home for night classes in the fall of 1968, my mother and I were having tea in our kitchen when we heard a frantic shout from upstairs, "Mrs. Kirwan! Call the police!"

We listened in the hallway to verify what we thought we had heard and immediately called for the police to respond. Mr. Hannigan, a sweet and thoughtful man when he was sober, was a violent and abusive husband when drunk. We would hear him verbally abusing his wife often in the evening, but when we'd see her the next day, she gave us no indication that there was a problem in her family.

When we heard Mrs. Hannigan cry out for help on that particular night, my mother sent me out to the front porch to direct the police up to the second-story apartment the moment they arrived. Thirteen-year-old Billy, the oldest son, had always appeared anxious. On this particular night he ran down the front stairs while his mother was still screaming. I reassured him that the Boston Police were on the way. Billy stood close to me on the porch, shaking and stuttering badly as he tried to tell me what was happening upstairs. His drunk father had lost control over his emotions and his fists. He beat his wife black and blue, and Billy had witnessed the assault.

Mrs. Hannigan momentarily had escaped her husband's clutches when he stopped his assault to refill his drink. In that moment, she yelled down to my mother and urged Billy to get out of the apartment. The younger children were either still sleeping or cowering in fear in their rooms from the commotion. I tried to calm Billy, but he voiced guilt over leaving his mother and siblings unprotected. He tried to run back up the stairs and I was forced to hold him back for the few more minutes it took until the police arrived.

Although it had only been a short period of time since my mother had called the police, it seemed to Billy and me that it was hours before the cruiser arrived. Billy's stuttering only worsened as he watched his father being led out of the house in handcuffs, while his mother clutched a handkerchief to cover her bruised face. Mrs. Hannigan's husband and batterer was taken away in the cruiser but held only for a brief "cooling down." Hours later, he returned home, somewhat more coherent and with his head hanging. His wife and children welcomed him back.

I didn't understand it at all. I didn't have any idea what to think. I had heard my father yell at my mother numerous times. He had shouted at most of us kids and hit us as punishment. I saw my cousins and friends' parents physically striking them as well for a variety of infractions. "Spankings" were such a common phenomenon that even on television situation comedies, it was routine for the fathers to put their wife or kids over their knees for a sound buttocks thrashing.

As a child, I didn't recognize that all of these were acts of violence. The subject of family abuse was not understood as a social problem, or one requiring the intervention of police until the early 1970s. Interestingly, when a soap opera introduced the issue of wife-battering in a story line, advertisers who sponsored production of the series pulled all of their funding.

The frantic request for my mother to call the police that evening had alerted us to trouble upstairs, but in our minds, what had occurred was a fight that had "gone too far." Domestic or family violence was not a crystallized concept to us at the time.

Mrs. Hannigan never acknowledged the incident to us, even though she had called my mother to help her. That didn't mean family violence stopped occurring in our realm. On another occasion not long after, Mrs. Hannigan was holding a small child for whom she was babysitting. As the second oldest in a family of then five children, as well as being a proficient babysitter for the children of relatives and neighbors, I could recognize an unhealthy child. Mrs. Hannigan was putting the toddler into a carriage when I noticed that the child was strangely pale, thinner than normal for her age, and had dark rings around her eyes.

I asked Mrs. Hannigan if the child was okay. She just answered, "She always looks like this. I don't know why." I felt deeply that something wasn't right with the toddler. I went inside and described what I had seen to my mother. She told me that she had seen the child too, but that it was not our business. I asked her why she had called the police when Mr. Hannigan had hurt his wife but was not intervening about this unhealthy-appearing child. My mother answered, "Because she asked for our help that night. She is not asking now."

I now know that I had unwittingly become part of what is defined as a culture of silence regarding family violence. People would see and hear threats and acts of intimidation and violence and believe that they should not interfere. Lack of clear-cut definitions and guidelines prevented police from acting uniformly when situations were outside of their jurisdiction.

But the family violence was not confined to 55 Edwin Street in Dorchester. It was a problem at the global level, the national level, the regional level, the local level, and in our own extended family. What is now considered domestic violence encompassed a wide range, from overly harsh punishment to threatening statements and actions, to lethal acts involving victims from infants to the elderly, pets, and police.

My parents firmly believed in the biblical admonition, "spare the rod, spoil the child." In our home, consequences for disobedience, fighting, or negative attitudes or language could vary from being yelled at or threatened, to slaps or being hit with my father's leather belt. If he felt that we had brought on his most severe punishment, my father would yank the belt through his pant's loops and snap it to get our attention. If we didn't capitulate to his power with an immediate apology, he struck with the belt. After the first lash, the one getting hit would beg him to stop. His children crying rendered him powerless, so my smarter sisters would start to cry as soon as he snapped the belt, and before even making contact with their tender skin. Hearing their pitiable cries, he'd immediately calm down, and then send them to their room. Within minutes, my father, chagrined himself, would go in to have a talk with the still weeping sisters. He'd always then apologize and hand them whatever cash he had in his pockets, by way of apology. Unfortunately, I was obstreperous from the start. If he struck me with the belt, I remained stoic. I would not cry for him. He'd hit me again, telling me why I deserved the strap. I'd say nothing. My mother, watching, would plead with me to apologize to him. I never did. He'd then give up and send me to my room. He'd later come to me with a fistful of cash along with plaintive pleas for me to understand why he "had" to strike me. I got lectures for why I had "deserved" to be hit. My facial expressions remained passive to his entreaties that I acquiesce to his superiority over me.

My mother also hit us, although nowhere near as often, and rarely with an object. She was more likely to threaten us with the ages-old warning to "wait until Dad gets home." That backfired as we began to dread him coming home, because when he did, and she revealed our misdeeds, we caught hell instead of a hello. It didn't endear our father to us.

The hitting stopped in my case when I was 16 years old. My mother had gotten really angry at me (likely because of my back-talk), and she raised a yardstick to strike me. I knew that I was wrong, but I felt that she was even more wrong to hit me. I instinctively grabbed the yardstick from her and broke it in half. I looked in her face and said, "Hitting is child abuse." She giggled nervously and said, "Yes, but it's allowed." I coldly said, "No, it isn't, and you will never put a hand on me again." She stopped. Later, my mother sat with us at tea and jokingly said, "You know? Parents are allowed to punish."

I informed her that laws were changing, and that now in 1970 the Massachusetts courts were characterizing acts of aggression, especially within the family, as "family violence." My mother, generally mild-mannered, tried to tease her way out of it and said, "Yes, but until now, it was legal." In all honesty, I believe that the majority of parents truly believed that they were shaping the behavior of their children by whatever means necessary, even if it involved striking them. To many parents, the degree of punishment was justified by the child's behaviors and attitudes.

Fortunately, society was beginning to shape attitudes otherwise with the promulgation of laws against family violence.

My father stopped hitting me in the same timeframe my mother did, but the circumstances were a bit more dramatic. I remember standing between my father and the stove when he came at me enraged for some infraction of his rules. I don't recall what it was, but I never really did anything deserving of being struck or screamed at. (It has been pointed out to me that even in making the above statement I still seem to indicate that something done to a victim was *provoked* by the victim. Now I can state with confidence that nothing that I ever did at home or elsewhere justified abuse.) Yet my father's bullying of me, in his view, was my own fault for saying or doing something that bothered him enough to hurt me. This is an all too common belief of victims of family violence. It is not hard to imagine that I had in fact talked back to him, as that always enraged him. It didn't take much, and he raised his fist to punch me.

I purposely reacted in a way that I knew was going to be a "make or break" moment. I *had* to make him stop, or he might break my bones. As he raised the fist and tried to strike me, I quickly reached up and grabbed his wrist. I put my face in his (as one might foolishly do with a rabid dog) and hissed, *"Don't even think of hitting me!"* His face turned purple with rage, and I would not let go. Time froze as I waited for his next move. But I got stronger just because he paused. To me, that signified him "blinking" and rethinking. He glared at me, but I held on to his wrist and glared back, certain that I had taken my own life in my hands. He slowly lowered his hand. He never hit me again.

I moved out of the house at 18, unaware that he continued to physically punish the younger kids and occasionally even slapped my mother. I didn't know it at the time, because I never saw it, but the family violence continued. His ill health at a very young age is likely what stopped his physical assaults, yet even when he became frail from severe heart disease, he would scream and tremble with rage if he believed any of us to be responsible for unacceptable behavior or attitudes. And yet I always loved him. It is a conundrum of family violence. Like many, "When he was good, he was very, very good, but when he was bad, he was horrid."

In much later years, I learned from cousins, particularly on my father's side of the family, that physical punishment had been ubiquitous throughout our extended family. It happened in many of my relatives' families, with the perpetrators predominantly the male parent and the primary victims the mothers and children.

Perpetrators' alcohol and drug abuse is a common contributing factor to family violence. In recent years, as I have reconnected with numerous cousins, we have discussed situations that we never shared as children. By the time (now) that we are in our 50s, 60s, and 70s, family members seem to want to forget old memories, deny them—or loudly acknowledge some ugly truths. It is important that not one family member has expressed anger, hatred, or rage for the abusive acts of (typically) their fathers. Most have softened, although not forgotten, the memories.

One comical, but understandable sentiment was expressed by an aunt with an ill-tempered husband about an event that occurred in the later years of their decades-long marriage. My aunt was a dedicated seamstress and crafter. I benefitted from some of her teachings, as she patiently demonstrated to me how to improve my sewing and crocheting.

One day, she was sitting downstairs at her sewing machine, thoroughly engrossed in a project. Suddenly it occurred to her that she hadn't seen her husband, who was at home, in a few hours. At a particularly challenging point in the task at hand, she was reluctant to put it down. She considered her husband's perplexing absence for a few moments, wondering if she should interrupt what she was doing and look for him. She pondered it for a moment, and later told her grown daughters that she decided to stay where she was and finish her work because, in her own words, "If Dad was dead, he'd still be dead in 20 minutes when I was planning on going upstairs anyway." At least one adult daughter found it uproariously funny, and also justifiable.

I learned in recent years that another respected uncle, to my shock, had often hit my feisty aunt. As their older children emerged into young adulthood, if Dad came home "in his cups" (intoxicated), he struck his wife. What surprised me the most about this, other than that he was a jovial and gentle fellow when sober, was that she had never retaliated and knocked him down a flight of stairs for laying a finger on her.

However, at a certain age, their older offspring recognized the indignities that their mother had suffered and refused to tolerate it anymore. If and when they were witness to Dad hitting their mother, three of them restrained him. If they deemed it necessary to stop his assaultive behavior, they struck their father to physically incapacitate him. This uncle managed somehow to wake up hangover-free, and memory-free as well. As he'd shave, he'd find that he had a fat lip, contusions and abrasions on his face and upper body, and sometimes split-open eyelids. Unashamed that he had no recall of any events of the preceding evening, he'd try to joke with his family, "Hey, anyone know how this happened to my face?" They would tell him. He would laughingly say, "Hey kids, next time go easy on me."

Matter-of-factly, they would reply that every time he struck their mother, they would overpower him and put him to bed. The couple still honored the "till death do us part" vow, although the family violence in itself had had the potential for bringing about that death prematurely.

I have told these stories of family violence with ambivalence. I recount them, unlike most of the stories in this book, not to entertain—but to reveal a seldom talked about facet of family life that was everywhere, to bear witness, and to give guidance to future generations.

37

❦

Dorchester in My Heart

As a family with more kids than bedrooms, we often slept two to a single bed. On rare occasions, we tripled up in a double bed, and I don't remember if this was by happenstance or choice. Either way, one Christmas morning when I was nine years old, Kathy, Jeanie, and I were all bundled together in my parents' old bed. Out of necessity, our dining room had been recently converted to sleeping quarters. Just through the folding double doors separating us from the parlor was our Christmas tree, and we were supposed to be slumbering until our parents announced that Santa had arrived. Only then could we come into the parlor to see what Santa had left for each of us. It was supposed to be a ceremonial event, with all of us gasping and shrieking together, not a bunch of heathens tearing into the mounds of ribbons and wrapping. (To my parents' chagrin, I had done just that on a previous Christmas, yelling, "*Hey*! I didn't want a train set!" only to be chastised for ripping open a gift with little Lonnie's name on the tag.)

We could get up when Mum and Dad announced that Santa had come during the night, leaving us with an abundance of good cheer, and never ever a piece of coal, as we had been threatened. We particularly feared the threat since my father, as an adolescent, had actually been the recipient of a piece of coal and no gifts whatsoever, after months of particularly pernicious behavior.

I strained my ears, listening for faraway jingling sleigh bells, or even a distant "Ho, ho, ho" as Santa dropped off presents for the other Dorchester families. I lay awake in the dark all night. Finally, a rummaging sound . . . and another . . . and whispering! Santa was here and only I knew! Kathy and Jeanie were in deep sleep, and I stayed still until the sweet sound of movement under and around our Christmas tree ceased. I crept out of the bed and opened just a crack the wooden folding doors separating our sleeping quarters from the parlor. I held my breath and peeked into the darkened room and beheld a bounty! A bit worried still about the coal, I stealthily slid one door aside on its track just enough to slip into the room.

It was all there! Santa had come and gone, and I spied with my little eyes packages that said "to Judy from Santa." I had to have them. (Story of my life. At nine years old, I knew that there was no Santa, but I decided each Christmas to suspend disbelief, on the off chance that he maybe did exist.) I crept into the parlor. Gingerly moving the array, I separated out a pile in which all the wrapped items had my name attached. I paused periodically to discern whether anyone else was awake. There was nothing but silence. Once I realized that everything left under the tree was for the rest of the family, I surreptitiously opened each of my gifts, trying to squelch my excitement. I had gotten through most of the pile when I heard Jeanie stir.

Hardly anything woke up Kathy. But Jeanie did. She shook Kathy and excitedly exclaimed that Santa had arrived. Both jumped out of bed and loudly joined me. Knowing that this did not portend a good outcome for me, as they quickly tore open their gifts, I sneakily moved my pile under the side of the bed where I was supposed to be sleeping. My mother awoke and unhappily came into the parlor. Trying to stay out of the fray as my mother focused on Jeanie and Kathy, I obediently climbed back into bed. Kathy, always happy that there was more time to sleep, did not put up much of a fuss and simply slid back under the covers. Jeanie had to be convinced by my mother that if she didn't go back to bed, Santa might send some of his elves to take away her gifts. She nearly vaulted over me in the bed, and squeezed her eyes shut, trying to convince my mother she was back in dreamland.

I snuggled under the covers with a smug look on my face. Still awake, I waited until I heard evidence that Jeanie and Kathy were, in fact, asleep, and that my mother had returned to bed.

Once everyone else went back to sleep, I slipped out of bed and sat on the floor. I quietly removed each of the still-wrapped packages from under the bed and spread them around me. This time I didn't wake anybody as I quietly stripped off all the wrapping and exclaimed softly over each of my gifts. But a harsh lesson was now to be learned. After I was truly tired out, I pushed my books and toys back under the bed and went to sleep. Before I knew it, there was a loud noise as the kids all ran into the parlor to open their gifts. They joyously held up and showed off each present to everyone gathered around the tree.

Only then did I understand my not so jolly folly. I had nothing to open. No surprises. I couldn't join in the revelry of Christmas morning amid all the wrappings and bows. I felt sad and I knew that it was my own fault. Nobody chastened me. Nobody had to. A lifelong lesson that I learned from Grandma Sadie (quoting Ben Franklin) struck home now: "He that can have patience can have what he will."

And how does this story form an ending to this book? My impatience caused me to ruin my own Christmas that one morning. That same feeling of impatience that I used to let rule my life was what I recall, moving out of Dorchester to South Weymouth. I was devastated, believing that I could never go back. In fact, we did go back to Dorchester that very day, to retrieve items that the movers had left behind. However, having to leave again before nightfall just reinforced my sorrows. Still possessing a severe lack of patience, I did not trust that I'd ever be back to Dorchester again.

Once in South Weymouth, we were only 18 or so miles to Boston. I discovered that various suburban bus routes connected with train routes and brought me to Ashmont Station. I could either walk throughout Dorchester to my planned destination, as I had always done, or take public transportation. For an OFD, we were used to walking until our shoe leather was paper thin. And as it turned out, faulty shoes were my ticket back to Dorchester almost immediately.

I entered ninth grade at South Junior High in South Weymouth, Massachusetts, in September of 1968. On the first day, I was dressed neatly for the occasion, wearing a navy jumper and yellow blouse, and a new pair of suede shoes that I had recently bought at Thom McAn in Fields Corner. The leather sole fell off in school—without my intervention! My heart exploded! I would not replace the shoes at South Shore Plaza; I insisted to my mother that I had to take the defective footwear back to the Thom McAn's where I had purchased them. She responded that I could certainly do that if I could find transportation. Within hours I had researched the means by which I would go the next day. I went to Dorchester, bringing a new friend from Weymouth with me. I had to show off where I had lived for all of my life. I was proud walking around my old neighborhood, but she looked askance at the humble surroundings, expressed dismay that there were sidewalks with curbs everywhere, and that litter lined the gutters of the streets. She turned her nose up at the proximity of the urban houses to each other, and dismissed all the chain link fencing, telling me that "no one in the suburbs fenced in their yards." That was the end of my new friendship. At least I had the courtesy to bring her back to South Weymouth.

But I still go back to Dorchester, over and over and over again.

It has been decades since I moved out of Dorchester, and yet I proudly wear my Dorchester and Boston Irish garb from College Hype on Gallivan Boulevard nearly every day. While I meander through Dorchester at least once a month—for me, Dorchester via Route I-93 is on the way to everywhere!—I also must stop at Greenhills Bakery for a supply of Irish soda bread, brown bread, scones, and beef stew.

At least once a year, I do my "main streets and back roads" trip, visiting all the homes where members of both sides of my family lived. Most moved out of Dorchester within the same time frame that my family did, but a few of the younger family members (including my sister's daughter Olivia) recently took up residence in the spacious apartments on Ashmont Hill.

I drive through Boston at least three times per week, visiting two of my daughters in Arlington and Watertown. Each time, I gaze upon the Rainbow Swash gas tank designed by Corita, an activist nun, who is believed to have incorporated an image of Ho Chi Minh within the blue stripe when she first painted the tank in the 1970s. The 140-foot-tall liquefied natural gas tank abuts expressway I-93 in Dorchester. It has been said to be the largest copyrighted work of art in the world. Highly visible to thousands of daily commuters, the Rainbow Swash is considered one of the major landmarks of Boston.

Remembering the words of Ben Franklin, it has been patience that allowed me to have "what I will." No matter where I call home, Dorchester will always be in my heart.

Notes

Chapter 2: Make Way for Mothering
The book *Make Way for Ducklings* by Robert McCloskey is the official children's book of the Commonwealth of Massachusetts. It has become such a symbol of Boston that the city in 1987 installed in a historic park a bronze of the entire brood of mother mallard and her babies—Jack, Kack, Lack, Mack, Nack, Ouack, Pack, and Quack—sculpted based on the drawings in the book. They are dressed in seasonal costumes, or even sports jerseys when the Boston Red Sox, New England Patriots, Boston Bruins, or Boston Celtics are enjoying winning seasons.

Chapter 13: Girls' Latin School and Society
Rampant racism and its results have continued to take place throughout my lifetime. The bulk of this chapter is focused on race relations in America from the late 1940s through the late 1960s. Information is also included about violence in the City of Boston both due to the anti-Vietnam War movement as well as continuing racial unrest when I was a student at Boston State College (September of 1974 through my graduation in May of 1976).

The civil rights movement was an organized effort by black Americans to end racial discrimination and gain equal legal rights. The movement is said to have originated in the late 1940s and gained traction during the 1950s and 1960s. Although turbulent at times, the movement was mostly nonviolent and was intended to result in laws to protect every American's constitutional rights, regardless of color, race, sex, or national origin. Decades later, that goal is yet to be satisfactorily attained.

The Maya Angelou quote in this chapter is from the video "Malcolm X Interview" published by the National Visionary Leadership Project, accessed on YouTube on August 24, 2020. https://www.youtube.com/watch?v=FcwZm5WuKdQ&list=PLCwE4GdJdVRL4B-iwUMfHH3zXOkPuNFcu

Chapter 30: Grandpa Tom and Grandma Sadie Currivan
The article quoted is from the November 12, 1938 *Boston Globe*.

About the Author

Judith Kirwan Kelley was born in Dorchester, Massachusetts in 1954, and lived there until the family joined in suburban migration, otherwise known as "white flight," in 1969. One of seven children in a typical Irish Catholic family, her relatives included, among others, Boston police officers, laborers, and housewives. Kirwan Kelley, a scholar with a Brown University PhD in Sociology, considers herself a lifetime creative writer. However, Kirwan Kelley's most valuable roles are as a socially conscious, married mother of three adult daughters, and Mimi to her six grandchildren. Storytelling has always been part of her life.

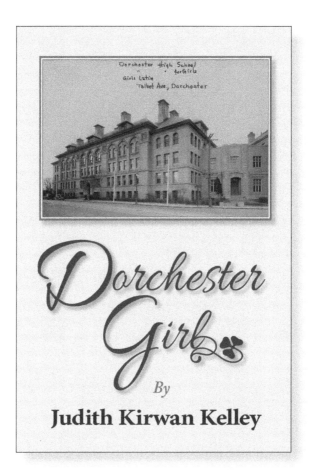

Dorchester Girl
Judith Kirwan Kelley

Publisher: SDP Publishing
Also available in ebook format

SDP Publishing

www.SDPPublishing.com
Contact us at: info@SDPPublishing.com

CPSIA information can be obtained
at www.ICGtesting.com
Printed in the USA
LVHW051100080122
708048LV00016B/1188

9 781736 199015